KU-241-484

CRISIS IN ENGLISH POETRY
1880 – 1940

English Literature

———————

Editor

PROFESSOR JOHN LAWLOR M.A.

Professor of English
in the University of Keele

BY THE SAME AUTHOR

CRITICISM AND BIOGRAPHY

Sir Charles Sedley
Peter Sterry, Platonist and Puritan
The English Renaissance (1510–1688)
Restoration Carnival
Enthusiast in Wit
William Blake

VERSE

The Invisible Sun
This is My England

TRANSLATIONS

The Road to the West
(with Alan Moray Williams)
The Wild Geese and Other Russian Fables

ANTHOLOGIES

The Common Muse
(Ed. with A. E. Rodway)
Poetry of the Restoration

CRISIS IN
ENGLISH POETRY
1880–1940

Vivian de Sola Pinto
MA, D.PHIL, FRSL
late Emeritus Professor of English,
University of Nottingham

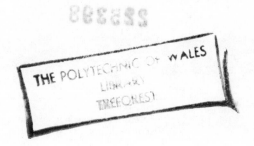
252393

THE POLYTECHNIC OF WALES
LIBRARY
TREFOREST

HUTCHINSON UNIVERSITY LIBRARY
LONDON

821.91209
PIN

820-1
"188/193"
(04/8)
PIN

HUTCHINSON & CO (*Publishers*) LTD
3 Fitzroy Square, London W1

London Melbourne Sydney Auckland
Wellington Johannesburg Cape Town
and agencies throughout the world

Published 1951
Second edition 1955
Third edition 1958
Fourth edition 1961
Reprinted 1965
Fifth edition 1967
Reprinted 1972

225398

The paperback edition of this book is sold subject to
the condition that it shall not, by way of trade or
otherwise, be lent, re-sold, hired out, or otherwise
circulated without the publisher's prior consent in
any form of binding or cover other than that in
which it is published and without a similar condition
including this condition being imposed on the
subsequent purchaser

© This edition V. de S. Pinto 1967

Printed in Great Britain by litho on smooth wove paper
by Anchor Press, and bound by Wm. Brendon,
both of Tiptree, Essex

ISBN 0 09 024411 7 (cased)
0 09 024412 5 (paper)

25/6/90

CONTENTS

In the past, Tradition, a kind of treaty of Versailles assigning frontiers and spheres of influence to the different interests, and based chiefly upon conquest, ordered our lives in a moderately satisfactory manner. But Tradition is weakening. Moral authorities are not as well backed by beliefs as they were; their sanctions are declining in force. We are in need of something to take the place of the old order. Not in need of a new balance of power, a new arrangement of conquests, but of a League of Nations for the moral ordering of the impulses; a new order based on conciliation, not on attempted suppression.

Only the rarest individuals hitherto have achieved this new order, and never yet perhaps completely. But many have achieved it for a brief while, for a particular phase of experience, and many have recorded it for these phases.

Of these records poetry consists.

I. A. RICHARDS, Science and Poetry (1926), p. 35.

. . . in cold Europe, in the middle of Autumn destruction,
Christopher stood, his face grown lined with wincing
In front of ignorance—'Tell the English,' he shivered,
        'Man is a spirit.'

W. H. AUDEN, The Orators (1930), p. 83.

PREFACE TO FIFTH EDITION

The publication of a fifth edition has provided me with an opportunity of making some alterations and additions. The most important of these are the rewriting of the passage on C. H. Sorley in Chapter 6, due partly to the useful criticism of Mr John Press, and the insertion in the same chapter of a brief account of David Jones's *In Parenthesis*, a work without reference to which I believe that not even the shortest survey of the poetry of the First World War can be regarded as complete. I acknowledge with thanks permission granted to me by Mr David Jones and Faber and Faber Ltd to make use of a quotation from *In Parenthesis*.

V. de S. Pinto

High Salvington, Worthing, January 1967

PREFACE

This book does not pretend to be a general history of English poetry in the period specified on the title page. It is designed solely as a study of the crisis in English poetry during those years and its relationship to the social, political and moral crisis of modern England. Certain well-known poets have only been mentioned casually and others have not been mentioned at all. This apparent neglect implies no judgment on the merit of their works. The book-lists appended to each chapter are not complete bibliographies but simply indications of some of the chief books which I have used and to which I think it may be useful to draw the attention of the reader. I take this opportunity of acknowledging my indebtedness to the following general works:

Edwin Muir: *The Present Age from 1914* (1939)
P. Henderson: *The Poet and Society* (1939)
Stephen Spender: *The Destructive Element* (1935)
C.M. Bowra: *The Heritage of Symbolism* (1943)
The Background of Modern Poetry (1946)
The Creative Experiment (1949)

F. R. Leavis: *New Bearings in English Poetry* (1932)
I. A. Richards: *Science and Poetry* (1926)
C. Day Lewis: *A Hope for Poetry* (7th ed. 1945)
                    The Poetic Image (1946)
Edmund Wilson: *Axel's Castle* (1936)
G. Bullough: *The Trend of Modern Poetry* (3rd. ed. 1949)
L. MacNeice: *Modern Poetry* (1938)
B. Ifor Evans: *English Poetry in the later Nineteenth Century*
                    (1933)
                    English Literature between the Two Wars (1948)
R. Graves and   *A Survey of Modernist Poetry* (1927)
Laura Riding:
J. Isaacs: *The Background of Modern Poetry* (1951)

My special thanks are due to my friends Basil Willey, L. A. G. Strong and D. S. R. Welland: the first for reading the whole work in typescript and suggesting numerous valuable corrections and improvements; the second for reading the chapter on *Yeats and Synge* and giving me excellent advice and criticism; and the third for allowing me to make use of his unpublished thesis on Wilfred Owen. I wish to acknowledge permission to quote certain poems in full, or in part, granted by the following publishers and owners of copyright: the Trustees of the Hardy Estate and Macmillan and Co Ltd for four poems from *The Collected Poems of Thomas Hardy* (Macmillan); Miss Margaret I. Carleton for two sonnets by Wilfred Scawen Blunt; the Oxford University Press for three poems by Gerard Manley Hopkins; Mr Walter de la Mare for his poem 'Echo'; Mr Siegfried Sassoon for his poem 'Blighters'; the representatives of J. M. Synge and George Allen and Unwin Ltd for a poem by J. M. Synge from his *Poems and Translations;* Mrs W. B. Yeats and Macmillan and Co Ltd for three poems from *The Collected Poems of W. B. Yeats* (Macmillan); Mr T. S. Eliot and Faber and Faber Ltd for extracts from Mr Eliot's poems; to Sidgwick and Jackson Ltd for extracts from Rupert Brooke's *Collected Poems;* the Society of Authors and Dr John Masefield, O.M., for passages from *The Collected Poems of John Masefield ;* Dr Edith Sitwell for passages from her *Collected Poems* and *The Canticle of the Rose.*

Nottingham, November 1950   V. de S. Pinto

INTRODUCTION

The crisis in English poetry which began about thirty years before
the outbreak of the First World War is a part of the moral,
intellectual, social and economic crisis of England and Western
Europe in which we are still living today. This crisis marks the end
of the great period of human history which began with the
Renaissance, and of which some of the chief aspects can be summed
up in the words of humanism, individualism, capitalism and
liberalism. During this period of about four hundred years England
was dominated by the families which carved out fortunes in the
confusion following the collapse of the Catholic feudal society of
the Middle Ages. They controlled the new weapon of money and
by means of it they curbed the monarchy and absorbed and
assimilated the remnants of the feudal aristocracy with which they
intermarried freely. These oligarchs succeeded in preserving some
elements of the courtly civilisation of the late Middle Ages and,
using them as a starting point, they created the society which produced the great tradition of English poetic culture, the tradition at
once Christian and humanistic that began with Sidney and Spenser
and ended with Tennyson and Bridges. It was the culture of a
leisured class living in spacious country houses in the midst of
gardens and parks, the great houses described by Evelyn in the
seventeenth century, which still formed the background of the
novels of Disraeli and Meredith in the nineteenth.

There had been a crisis in English poetry in the fifteenth century
when medieval civilization foundered in the dynastic wars and no
new poet appeared capable of developing Chaucer's splendid veins
of realism and humour and Langland's powerful and vivid criticism
of society; but the new culture of the triumphant oligarchs of the
sixteenth century, such as the Russells, the Sidneys, the Sackvilles,
and the Cecils, re-established the tradition after the end of the Wars
of the Roses. Wyatt and Surrey renewed the contact with Italian
humanism which had already stimulated Chaucer at the end of the
fourteenth centruy. Spenser, the first great poet of the revival
proclaimed significantly that the object of his masterpiece was
'To fashion a gentleman or noble person in vertuous and gentle
discipline.' The new poetry of the sixteenth century was the

poetry of the courtier, the cultivated gentleman of leisure, and English poetry of the central tradition never lost sight of Spenser's ideal. The poetry belonging to this tradition is based ultimately on an agricultural community, on the life of the earth and the rhythm of the seasons, and on an aristocratic, but, on the whole, liberal and kindly society, resting on family loyalties and a personal relationship between landlord and tenant and master and servant. This poetry has great variety but its typical products are in smooth, flowing rhythms, 'the liquid diction, the fluid movement', which Matthew Arnold traced from Chaucer to Spenser, Shakespeare, Milton and Keats. Besides this central Apollonian or Bardic tradition there was also a tradition of colloquial, realistic poetry, the sort of poetry which, to use the words applied by Arnold to Burns, is characterized by 'spring, bounding swiftness' rather than fluidity; it can be traced from the medieval ballads to Skelton and the Elizabethan and Stuart broadsides. The Elizabethan dramatists were heirs to both traditions, and, at the great creative movement of the English Renaissance, in Marlowe, Shakespeare and Jonson, there was a successful fusion between the 'Apollonian' poetry of the court and the 'Dionysian' poetry of the people. The same fusion is to be found on a smaller scale in the best work of the metaphysical poets Donne, Herbert and Marvell, who took over from the dramatists the use of colloquial diction and conversational rhythms and combined them with learning and courtly grace. In the seventeenth century, however, a spiritual disintegration was already beginning. One aspect of it was the division of poetry into 'polite' or bardic verse in 'poetic diction' and popular verse in colloquial diction, now considered suitable only for light or comic themes. Another aspect was that separation of poetic thought from poetic feeling which T. S. Eliot has noted as beginning in the age of Dryden. There is little doubt that both these types of 'dissocia-tion' were connected with the weakening of the alliance between poetry and the governing class. This alliance became more and more difficult to maintain in the three centuries that separate Spenser from Tennyson, as the old courtly tradition of Christian humanism faded and the oligarchy became more and more com-mercialized, demanding from the poet instead of art either amuse-ment or instruction. In *The Princess* (1847) Tennyson shows us a progressive squire giving up his 'broad lawns until the set of sun' to 'the people'. The vision of an England with a happy contented population led by a beneficent class of enlightened squires and manufacturers did not seem extravagant in 1847. In the latter half of the century, however, technical invention and industrial development transformed the face of England, which became covered with factories, slums and ugly, unplanned, sprawling suburbs. Beside Tennyson's vision of Sir Walter Vivian's park we can place George Gissing's picture of North London in *Demos* (1886); 'To walk about in such a neighbourhood as this is the dreariest exercise to which a man can betake himself; the heart is crushed by uniformity decent squalor; one remembers that each of these dead-faced houses, often each separate blind-window, represents a "home" and the associations of the word whisper blank despair.' In the landscape of *The Princess* there is still a place for the poet; he is the guest of Sir Walter Vivian enjoying the spacious life of the country house, and making poetry out of the fete which symbolises the alliance of upper class culture with industry. But in George Gissing's landscape of the industrialised England of the 'eighties there is no place where a poet could be happy. As Professor Trevelyan writes, 'the race bred under such conditions might retain many sturdy qualities of character, might even with better food and clothing, improve in physique, might develop sharp wits and a brave, cheery, humorous attitude to life but its imaginative powers must necessarily decline, and the stage is set for the gradual standardisation of human personality'.

Standardisation and uniformity have been noted by Arnold Toynbee as marks of the period of 'the schism in the soul' which heralds the decay of civilization. Late nineteenth-century critics often expressed surprise that no 'great' new poet appeared as a successor to Tennyson and Browning. If by a 'great' poet was meant a poet whose work represented the equilibrium of a society that had achieved some degree of integration, it was impossible for Tennyson to have a successor of this kind, as such an equilibrium no longer existed after about 1880. If poetry was to be kept alive, it was useless to try to repeat the success of Tennyson or any other Victorian poet. A new kind of poetry was needed to express that 'schism in the soul' which is the most significant fact in the modern world, and, at the same time, to attempt the supremely difficult task of overcoming it and creating a new spiritual integration, thus defying, at any rate on the imaginative plane, the process of standardisation which was proceeding rapidly in an industrialized society.

I

THE TWO VOYAGES

I

C. F. G. Masterman in his *Condition of England*, published in 1909, defined the possibilities for the writers of his time as 'two voyages': 'a voyage without in the actual encounter with primitive and hostile forces and in a universe of salt and bracing challenges; and a voyage within and across distant horizons and to stranger countries than any visible to the actual senses'. If he had written twenty years later, he would doubtless have used the jargon of modern psychology and spoken of the writing of 'extroverts' and 'introverts'. The greatness of the English poetry of the past has consisted to a large extent in the way in which it succeeded in harmonising the claims of the inner and the outer life. 'Balance', wrote that acute critic Demetrios Capetanakis, 'is the secret of the English genius. English is the creation neither of the body nor the spirit alone, but of both'. Chaucer, Spenser, Marlowe, Shakespeare, Donne, Milton, Pope, Wordsworth, Keats, Tennyson and Browning all succeeded in making both 'voyages'. All were explorers both of the outer and of the inner world; their feet are firmly planted on the earth, and yet their minds are for ever 'voyaging through strange seas of thought alone'. They could be 'realistic' in their poetry because the world around them, in spite of many shortcomings, was not hostile to poetry, and they could be meditative and introspective because their inner life was enriched by a great and living poetic tradition. Somewhere about the year 1880 this state of affairs ceased to exist. The Pre-Raphaelites of 1848-56 had instinctively foreseen the coming crisis and had tried to carry out an aesthetic revolution, which would at once anticipate it and overcome it. They failed because they underestimated the forces which were opposed to them and misunderstood their nature:

George Meredith, in his last novel, compared the English poets, as they were in his old age, to the 'Celts', the Irish, Welsh and Gaelic Scots, who had no love for John Bull:

> They are in the Celtic dilemma of standing at variance with Bull; they return him his hearty antipathy, are unable to be epical or lyrical of him, are condemned to expend their genius on the abstract, the quaint, the picturesque. Nature they read spiritually or sensually, always shrinkingly apart from him. They swell to a resemblance of their patron if they stoop to woo his purse. He had, on hearing how that poets being praise to nations, as in fact he can now see his Shakespeare to have done, been seen to thump the midriff and rally them for their shyness of it, telling them he doubts them true poets while they abstain from singing him to the world—him, and the things refreshing the centre of him. Ineffectual is that encouragement.

Verlaine in the Prologue to his *Poèmes Saturniens* said almost the same thing:

> Aujourd'hui, l'Action et le Rêve ont brisé
> Le pacte primitif par les siècles usé,
> Et plusieurs ont trouvé funeste ce divorce
> De l'harmonie immense et bleue et de la Force.
> .   .   .   .
> Cependant orgueilleux et doux loin des vacarmes
> De la vie et du choc désordonné des armes
> Mercenaires voyez, gravissant les hauteurs
> Ineffables, voici le groupe des Chanteurs
> Vêtus de blanc. . . .
> Le monde, que troublait leur parole profonde,
> Les exile. À leur tour ils exilent le monde![1]

Both Meredith and Verlaine are thinking of the poets of their time who chose the 'voyage within', deliberately cutting themselves off from the life of the common man in order to dedicate their lives to a purely aesthetic ideal. In England, these were the poets and artists who became known as 'decadents', and whom W. B. Yeats, who

---

[1] 'Today Action and Dream have broken their ancient pact, which has been worn out by the centuries, and some have seen a terrible significance in this divorce between the great blue Harmony and Strength. . . . Nevertheless, proud and gentle, far from the hubbub of life and the disorderly shock of mercenary arms, behold, ascending ineffable heights, the group of Singers clad in white. . . . The World, which their profound words have troubled, banishes them. They, in their turn, banish the World.'

was himself one of them in his youth, called the 'tragic generation': Oscar Wilde, Ernest Dowson, Lionel Johnson, Aubrey Beardsley, Arthur Symons and Theodore Wratislaw. These poets were the literary descendants of the Pre-Raphaelites and especially of Swinburne. They had no interest, however, in the medievalism of Rossetti and Morris, or in Swinburne's Hellenism or his politics. It was the Swinburne of 'Dolores' and 'Faustine' rather than the Swinburne of *Atalanta* or *Songs before Sunrise* who interested them, and they followed Swinburne in their admiration for contemporary French poetry. They were more European in their outlook than any group of English poets since the Restoration Wits and all of them were as much at home in Paris as in London. At the end of the nineteenth century the great French symbolist movement dominated European poetry as completely as Anglo-German romanticism had dominated it in the age of Goethe and Byron. To Swinburne's admiration of Baudelaire and Gautier his young English disciples added a cult of Verlaine, the picturesque old bohemian who had lived in London in his youth and was one of the sights of Paris in the eighteen-nineties. Only Arthur Symons and his young Irish friend W. B. Yeats seem to have extended their studies to the more difficult and esoteric poetry of Stephane Mallarmé, the high priest of Symbolism and to Laforgue and Rimbaud, whose works had little or no influence in England before the twentieth century.

Oscar Wilde (1856–1900) is connected with the group and yet stands apart from it. Unlike the others he was an 'extravert'. So far from 'banishing the world' or being banished by it, he was a wit and a showman who loved popularity and worldly success. A pupil of Walter Pater at Oxford, he applied Pater's aesthetic philosophy in exactly the way that Pater must have feared that it would be applied when he suppressed the famous epilogue to *The Renaissance*. In the days of his prosperity he dominated the London dinner tables by his conversation and the London theatres by the sparkling wit of his comedies. As Yeats wrote, 'he must humour and cajole and pose, take worn out stage situations, for he knows that he may be as romantic as he pleases so long as he does not believe in romance'. The poet in Wilde was half stifled by the showman and the journalist and stunted by a hedonism which mistook pleasure for beauty and decoration for art. Unfortunately, by the conventions of his time his admirable Irish wit and humour were excluded from his verses, which for the most part are as meretricious as artificial jewellery, mere *pastiches* of the English romantic poets, the Pre-Raphaelites and contemporary French poetry. The most interesting of his early poems is the pathetic sonnet which is a prophecy of his whole career:

> To drift with every passion till my soul
> Is a stringed lute on which all lutes can play,
> Is it for this that I have given away
> Mine ancient wisdom, and austere control?

There is generally more poetry in his prose than in his verse, and the best poem that he wrote before his imprisonment is the prose Hymn to Art prefixed to *The Picture of Dorian Gray*, a comment on life as penetrating as that of Blake's *Heaven and Hell* or Nietzsche's *Zarathustra*:

The nineteenth century dislike of Realism is the rage of Caliban seeing his own face in a glass. The nineteenth century dislike of Romanticism is the rage of Caliban not seeing his own face in a glass.
. . . . .

All art is at once surface and symbol. Those who go beneath the surface do so at their peril. Those who read the symbol do so at their peril. It is the spectator, and not life that art really mirrors.

The Ballad of Reading Gaol, begun when he was in prison in 1895, is different from any of his other poems. Here for once he 'goes beneath the surface at his peril'. Although the *Ballad* echoes Coleridge's *Ancient Mariner* and A. E. Housman's recently published *Shropshire Lad*, it is a truly original work. This poem is not merely a vivid picture of the sordid misery of the later Victorian English gaol. The prison and the condemned guardsman are symbols and the poem is a memorable and effective 'reading of the symbols', an expression of the guilt of a society which shut its eyes to the horror of the penal system.

> For each man kills the thing he loves,
> Yet each man does not die.
>
> He does not die a death of shame
> On a day of dark disgrace,
> Nor have a noose about his neck
> Nor a cloth upon his face,
> Nor drop feet foremost through the floor
> Into an empty space.

> He does not wake at dawn to see
> Dread figures throng his room,
> The shivering Chaplain robed in white,
> The Sheriff stern with gloom,
> And the Governor all in shiny black,
> With the yellow face of Doom.

The Ballad of Reading Gaol and the essay on 'The Soul of Man Under Socialism' suggest that if Wilde could have outgrown the shallow hedonism, which he mistook for a philosophy of art, he might have become the poet of the awakening social conscience of his age.

The poets of the Rhymers' Club, who met at the Cheshire Cheese in the eighteen-nineties, and contributed to *The Yellow Book*, *The Savoy* and *The Century Hobby Horse*, were much nearer than Wilde to Verlaine's conception of a group of singers banished by the world and banishing the world. These writers, Ernest Dowson, Lionel Johnson, W. B. Yeats, Arthur Symons, Theodore Wratislaw and others, deliberately cut themselves off from the common life of late Victorian England, making it, in Yeat's words, 'a matter of conscience to turn from every kind of money-making that prevented good writing' and to cultivate 'emotion which had no relation to any public interest'. For them art was a kind of religion, but none of them except Yeats had the courage to devote himself to that religion with the wholehearted integrity of a Mallarmé or the wild ecstasy of a Rimbaud; Dowson, Johnson and their friends too rarely 'went beneath the surface' or attempted to 'read the symbol'. Their aim was that of Mallarmé: to create a new poetic language by means of an intense cultivation of the inner life:

> Donner un sens plus pur aux mots de la tribu.

To achieve this aim, a concentration of purpose beyond the strength of most of the Rhymers was necessary. Ernest Dowson (1867–1900) has been the most highly praised among them. He is a kind of small Verlaine with all Verlaine's vagueness and gentleness and something too of Verlaine's exquisite gift of word music, but his poetry has a narrower range than Verlaine's, and far less humanity and versatility. Dowson's verse is full of nostalgia and wistfulness and what Yeats calls 'a slight sentimental sensuality'. His most famous poem 'Non Sum Qualis Eram Bonae Sub Regno Cynarae' has an original and attractive metrical movement:

I have forgot much, Cynara! gone with the wind,
Flung roses, roses riotously with the throng,
Dancing, to put thy pale, lost lilies out of mind. . . .

The roses and lilies of this passage certainly come from Swinburne's 'Dolores'; they are bookish, hackneyed images bearing no
vital relationship to the squalid dissipation of Soho in the eighteen-
nineties. Indeed, much of Dowson's poetry is the result not of an
exploration of the inner life but of wistful day-dreaming. However,
'Non Sum Qualis Eram' is notable as an expression of the unhap-
piness of the poet and his sense of the emptiness of the world in
which he lived, but, like much of Dowson's writing, it is marred by
self pity and the attempt to romanticise the squalid and second rate.
The madman in the sonnet, 'To One in Bedlam', is, perhaps, a
more appropriate and successful symbol of Dowson's poetic ideal.

With delicate, mad hands behind his sordid bars,
Surely he hath his posies, which they tear and twine;
Those scentless wisps of straw that miserably line
His straight, caged universe, whereat the dull world stares,
Pedant and pitiful. O how his rapt gaze wars
With their stupidity! Know they what dreams divine
Lift his long, laughing reveries like enchaunted wine,
And make his melancholy germane to the stars.

Professor Tillotson has drawn attention to Dowson's originality
as a metrist and to the 'loosening of rhythm and loosening of
syntax' of which hints appear in his writings. He is too fond of
traditional images such as wine, roses, stars, and moonlight and his
diction for the most part is a pale and flaccid imitation of Swinburne's. The sights and sounds of contemporary London are
excluded from his poetry, but there is no vision of a symbolic
reality to take their place. At its worst, his verses can be almost as
trivial and imbecile as those of Richard Le Gallienne, the weakest
of the Rhymers.

Lionel Johnson (1867–1902) is much more intellectual and
scholarly and much less vague and dreamy than Dowson. His
poetry is not haunted as Dowson's is by the romantic pseudo-
personality of the melancholy, misunderstood young poet-lover.
This pseudo-personality haunted English poetry for some time, and
imitation Dowsons continued to publish slim volumes of verse well
into the twentieth century. Johnson was a brilliant scholar of

Winchester College and New College, Oxford, and one of his
weaknesses is that he is perpetually brooding over the august
traditions of those famous seats of learning. His poems on Oxford
and Winchester are impeccable pieces of conventional craftsmanship, but they are too much like the prize poems of a supernaturally
clever public schoolboy. In them, he says all the right things, in
lucid, melodious language and perfectly chiselled verse. Gray and
Arnold are his masters in these poems rather than Baudelaire or
Verlaine. Indeed, if Verlaine had seen them he might well have
used the words that he applied to Tennyson: 'il est trop noble,
trop anglais'. But Johnson has other experiences besides those of
the scholar of Winchester and New College. Sometimes he writes
as a romantic Tory and Jacobite ('Mystic and Cavalier'), a figure
popularised by Shorthouse's *John Inglesant* (1880), and sometimes
as a Celtic revivalist brooding over the immemorial traditions of
Wales, Cornwall or Ireland. Unfortunately for his reputation the
anthologists have nearly always chosen to represent him by his vague,
sentimental poem on King Charles' Statue at Charing Cross, one
of the least satisfactory products of the 'mystic and cavalier' Johnson.
In one remarkable poem, Johnson 'went below the surface' and
expressed his intuition of the terror that haunted the emptiness of
the aesthetic Palace of Art,

> Dark Angel, with thine aching lust,
> To rid the world of penitence:
> Malicious Angel, who still dost
> My soul such subtile violence!
> . . . .
>
> When music sounds, then changest thou
> Its silvery to a sultry fire:
> Nor will thy envious heart allow
> Delight untortured by desire.
>
> Through thee, the gracious Muses turn
> To Furies, O mine Enemy!
> And all the things of beauty burn
> With flames of evil ecstasy.

In the glowing sonnet on the anabaptists of Munster (*Munster:
A.D. 1534*) Johnson gives a hint of the magnificence of vision
which he might have achieved if he had been less encumbered by
academic convention and good taste:

> We are the golden men, who shall the people save:
> For only ours are visions, perfect and divine;

For we alone are drunken of the last, best wine;
And very Truth our souls hath flooded, wave on wave.
Come wretched death's inheritors, who dread the grave!
Come! for upon our brows is set the starry sign
Of prophet, priest and king: star of the lion line:
Leave Abana, leave Pharpar, and in Jordan lave!

The designer and illustrator, Aubrey Beardsley (1872–1898), though he only wrote a few copies of verse and a fragment of a story of poetic prose, has a place in the history of the poets of the 'tragic generation'. More fearlessly than any of the Rhymers, he explored the depths of late Victorian mind and in his drawings and his prose story expresses the vision of evil which they usually avoided or obscured with sentimental fantasies. As Osbert Burdett has written, 'the corruption of the soul that he depicted was no nightmare of a disordered imagination. The pretension of health was the fantastic dream. To give outline and definition to the sense of corruption, to recover the vision of evil, was a sign of healthy vitality in his work'.

He illustrated Dowson's play *The Pierrot of the Minute*, but his own satiric designs such as 'The Wagnerites' and 'Lady Gold's Escort' are criticisms of his age far beyond Dowson's powers. In his original poem 'The Three Musicians' he uses realistic material with the delicate precision of his drawings and with an irony that is a refreshing contrast to the 'slight sentimental sensuality of' his friends:

One's a soprano, lightly frocked
In cool, white muslin that just shows
Her brown silk stockings gaily clocked,
Plump arms and elbows tipped with rose,
And frills of petticoats and things, and outlines as the
    warm wind blows.

Beside her a slim, gracious boy
Hastens to mend her tresses' fall,
And dies her favour to enjoy,
And dies for *réclame* and recall
At Paris and St Petersburg, Vienna and St James's Hall.

John Davidson was right when he said that the Rhymers lacked 'blood and guts'. They were too timid, too cloistered, too pedantic and too self-consciously Bohemian to make that thorough exploration of the inner life which was the necessary prelude to any rebuilding of English poetry. Most of them can be described as tourists rather than explorers. Only one of them had the courage and intellectual integrity to carry through the adventure of the 'voyage within' to its logical conclusion. This was the young Irishman, William Butler Yeats. Davidson admitted that this Rhymer had 'blood and guts' and he was right if he meant, not that Yeats would write energetic 'popular' poetry, but that he was capable of exploring the empty but haunted regions of the late Victorian Palace of Art without becoming a sexual pervert, or drinking himself to death, and of proceeding with an enriched experience and unimpaired creative power to a more universal and enduring kind of art.

The Rhymers have a small place in the history of English poetry in virtue of their own achievement. They are also worthy of remembrance because of the important part which they played in the education of a great poet.

II

The period 1880–1900 was the age of realism and impressionism in European prose fiction and painting. It was the age of Zola and Maupassant, of George Moore and George Gissing, of the French impressionist painters and their disciples of the New English Art Club. It was inevitable that there should be a realistic poetry in such a period, especially in a country like England, where the life of action was always admired, and where there was an old tradition of a poetry of physical energy and the open air, going back to Chaucer and the medieval ballads, and embodied more recently in the work of Scott, Byron and Browning.

Three poets during this period made a determined effort to renew the pact between Action and Dream,[1] which Verlaine declared had been broken in his time. One of the three was himself a man of action, an aristocrat, a great traveller, and a political rebel; the other two were journalists whose work brought them into close touch with those worlds of politics and business that were shunned by the introverted poets of the 'tragic generation'.

Wilfred Scawen Blunt (1840–1922), the oldest of the three, is a poet whose work has been unjustly neglected, probably because of his political opinions. He was the last of the English gentleman poets, a rebellious aristocrat like Ralegh, Rochester and Byron.

[1] See above, p. 14.

The Blunts were an ancient Roman Catholic family of Sussex landowners, and Wilfred Blunt at an early age entered the pleasant
leisurely world of Victorian diplomacy. He served as an attaché
at various British Embassies and Legations, Athens, Constantinople,
Frankfurt, Madrid and Paris. It was in the France of the Second
Empire that he met the brilliant courtesan 'Skittles', who inspired
some of the best of his early poetry. This early poetry of Blunt,
consisting of the sonnet sequences, *Esther* and *Proteus*, the novel in
rhymed verse, *Griselda*, and some shorter pieces, is a splendid
record of a cosmopolitan upper class society free from the
puritanism and insularity of Victorian England. 'He writes throughout as one in and of a certain *monde*, as a man about town, a *viveur*
(the term is used in no illiberal sense), a country gentleman who is
also a person in society; so that his poetry has a savour and an
impulse which make it a thing apart in modern verse.'[1] The style
of Blunt's early poems is remarkably pure, yet easy and colloquial,
owing much to Byron for whose work he had an unbounded
admiration. Although Blunt was a Catholic by birth and upbring-
ing, his early poetry is an expression of the healthy paganism of
the English Victorian aristocrat. The great sonnet sequence *To
Esther* is a record of his own liaison with Skittles: there is no trace
of sordidness or affectation in this frank, powerful narrative. The
man's intellectual honesty, his clean sensuality and his enormous
zest for life make it one of the impressive poems of its age and for
a moment in the two great sonnets that celebrate the rapture of
his love, he achieves a synthesis of thought and passion which is
Elizabethan rather than Victorian.

> When I hear laughter from a tavern door,
> When I see crowds agape and in the rain
> Watching on tiptoes and with stifled roar
> To see a rocket fired or a bull slain,
> When misers handle gold, when orators
> Touch strong men's hearts with glory till they weep,
> When cities deck their streets for barren wars
> Which have laid waste their youth, and when I keep
> Calmly the count of my own life, and see
> On what poor stuff my manhood's dreams were fed
> Till I too learned what dole of vanity,
> Will serve a human soul for daily bread,
> —Then I remember that I once was young
> And lived with Esther the world's Gods among.

[1] W. E. Henley, preface to *The Poetry of Wilfred Blunt* (1898).

There is the same rapture and the same simplicity in some of the poems that are inspired by the joy of movement in the open air.

> To-day, all day I rode upon the Down,
> With hounds and horsemen, a brave company.
> On this side in its glory lay the sea,
> On that the Sussex Weald, a sea of brown.
> The wind was light, and brightly the sun shone
> And still we galloped on from gorse to gorse
> And once, when checked, a thrush sang and my horse
> Pricked his quick ears as to a sound unknown.
> I knew the Spring was come. I knew it even
> Better than all by this that through my chase
> In bush and stone and hill and sea and heaven
> I seemed to see and follow still your face.
> Your face my quarry was. For it, I rode,
> My horse a thing of wings, myself a God.

These early poems of Blunt are the work of a gentleman of rank and fashion whose poetry is part of his life and who can write in a completely unaffected way about his loves, his delight of Nature, partridge shooting, dinners at the Maison D'Or in Paris, and debates in the House of Commons. This poet is a member of a governing class which still accepts poetry as a normal part of its existence, a class in which a gentleman finds it as natural to write a sonnet as to ride to hounds, dine at his club, or take part in a parliamentary debate. Blunt was the last considerable poet produced by that society. It was dying in 1880[1] and it is highly significant that Blunt found it impossible to continue to live and write in the world of gentlemanly leisure. He found two ways of escape, one through his travels in the east and the other through political revolt.

He married Lady Anne Blunt, Byron's grand-daughter and travelled with her through Arabia. They studied Arabic poetry together and in it Blunt found a new inspiration. For him the east is not a luxurious dream-world of pleasure as it was for the poets of the romantic age but the home of manly loyalties and a life led in harmony with nature. *The Seven Golden Odes of Arabia* and the short epic in mixed prose and verse called *The Stealing of the Mare* are adaptations of Arabic poems which have the quality of original works and their unrhymed metres are Blunt's most interesting contribution to English prosody:

[1] Henry James in *The Princess Casamasssima* (1886) describes English upper class society at that date as 'the deadness of the grave'.

Alas for the dark-lipped one, the maid of the topazes,
  hardly yet a grown woman, sweet fruit-picking loiterer!
A girl, a fawn still fawnless, which browses the thorn-bushes,
  close to the doe-herd feeding, aloof in the long valleys.
I see her mouth-slit smiling, her teeth—nay a camomile
  white on the white sand blooming, and moist with the night-showers.
Sun-steeped it is, pure argent, white all but the lips of her,
  these too are darkly painted to shrink from the sun-burning.
The face of her now joyous, the day's robe enfolding her,
  clean as a thing fresh fashioned, untouched by sad time-fingers.

Like Browning, Blunt found poetry in nations whose sensibility had not been debased by western civilisation. But his oriental poems are a sort of *tour de force* like Fitzgerald's *Omar Khayyam*, and too remote in their themes and their imagery from English life to affect the main tradition of English poetry.

Blunt's moral sensibility was deeply wounded by the greed and cruelty and vulgarity of the new imperialism which became the fashionable creed of the English upper class in the late nineteenth century. He started by championing the Irish Land League and was imprisoned in Galway gaol in 1887. Then he adopted the cause of the Egyptian Nationalist leader Arabi and devoted a large part of his energy in the later years of his life to a campaign against British imperialism in every part of the world. He tried to make poetry out of his generous indignation on behalf of the victims of imperialism but the matter was intractable and his political poetry is only moderately successful. His first attempt was in the form of the sonnet-sequence which he had used so admirably for love poetry. The series of sonnets called *In Vinculis* written in Galway gaol is dignified and pathetic but contains no really weighty or memorable poem. The bitter and sombre monologue, 'The Canon of Aughrim', is much more successful. It is a poem of the sort that Browning might have written if he had interested himself in Irish politics instead of those of Italy. Blunt's most impressive political poem is certainly the passionate indictment of British policy in Egypt called 'The Wind and the Whirlwind' (1883).

The Empire thou didst build shall be divided.
  Thou shalt weighed be in thine own balances
Of usury to peoples and to princes,
  And be found wanting by the world and these.

They shall possess the lands by thee forsaken
  And not regret thee. On their seas no more

> Thy ships shall bear destruction to the nations,
>   Or thy guns thunder on a fenceless shore.
>
> Thou hadst no pity in thy day of triumph.
>   These shall not pity thee. The world shall move,
> On its high course and leave thee to thy silence,
>   Scorned by the creatures that thou couldst not love.

This poem has a rush and a vigour that recalls Swinburne, whose poetry Blunt greatly admired. It also has a quality of abstract and empty rhetoric like that of Swinburne's fulminations in *Songs before Sunrise*. Blunt's indignation is noble and sincere but his sensibility is not sufficiently rich to provide an adequate expression for it. His most ambitious work was the short philosophic epic called *Satan Absolved* in which he collaborated with the old philosopher, Herbert Spencer. This is a dialogue between God and Satan based on the book of Job. Satan's great speech in which he arraigns humanity, and especially the Anglo-Saxon world is the culmination of Blunt's work, a memorable expression of the poet's revolt against the ugliness and meanness of an industrialised age:

> The smoke of their foul dens
> Broodeth on Thy fair Earth as a black pestilence,
> Hiding the kind day's eye. No flower, no grass there groweth,
> Only their engines' dung which the fierce furnace throweth.
> Their presence poisoneth all and maketh all unclean.
> Thy streams they have made sewers for their dyes aniline,
> No fish therein may swim, no frog, no worm, may crawl,
> No snail for grime may build her house within their wall.
> Thy beasts they have enslaved in blindness underground,
> The voice of birds that sang to them is a lost sound.
>   .   .   .   .
>
> These Lords who boast Thine aid at their high civic feasts,
> The ignoble shouting crowds, the prophets of their Press,
> Pouring their daily flood of bald self-righteousness,
> Their poets who write big of the 'White Burden'. Trash!
> The White Man's Burden, Lord, is the burden of his cash.

This is the protest of a representative of a dying civilisation against the ugliness of a world which he cannot understand. There is nobility in the protest but it is sterile and uncreative. The unsatisfactory mixture of archaism and colloquialism in the diction is a measure of the failure of the poet to give adequate expression to the modern 'Schism in the Soul'. Blunt hates the ugliness of the modern world but he cannot master it and transform it into poetic material.

William Ernest Henley (1849–1903), an admirer of Blunt's writings and editor of an excellent selection from his poems, was an important pioneer of the new realism in English poetry. The son of a Gloucester bookseller, he had the advantage of a stimulating education under T. E. Brown, the Manx poet, at Gloucester Crypt Grammar School. His first memorable poetry was the result of his experience at the Edinburgh Infirmary where he underwent an operation and was the patient of Lister for twenty months (1873–5). The series of lyrics and sonnets first published as *Hospital Outlines* in the Cornhill Magazine (XXXII, 1875) and included in his collected poems, under the title *In Hospital*, is one of the starting points of the English poetry of the modern crisis. It is highly significant that the subject of these poems is a hospital, the symbol both of the sickness of the modern world and its preoccupation with science:

> A tragic meanness seems so to environ
> These corridors and stairs of stone and iron,
> Cold, naked, clean—half work-house and half-jail.

These poems are, perhaps, the first resolute attempt in English to use ugliness, meanness and pain as subjects of poetry. Browning, indeed, had experimented in the use of ugliness, but in his work it was always picturesque or grotesque and combined with some sort of moralising explicit or implied. Henley's hospital poems are, perhaps, the first in which an English poet finds completely satisfactory images in the kind of ugliness peculiar to the modern world:

> As with varnish red and glistening,
> Dripped his hair; his feet looked rigid;
> Raised, he settled stiffly sideways:
> You could see his hurts were spinal.
>
> He had fallen from an engine,
> And been dragged along the metals.
> It was hopeless, and they knew it;
> So they covered him and left him.
>
> As he lay by fits half sentient,
> Inarticulately moaning,
> With his stockinged soles protruded
> Stark and awkward from the blankets. . . .

Henley's unrhymed metres are descended from those of Heine,
by whose work he was profoundly influenced; nevertheless they
are different from Heine's and the best of them, in spite of dates,
belong to the twentieth rather than to the nineteenth century. In a
few poems he created irregular rhythms which are really expressive
of the uprooted and divided modern consciousness:

> A desolate shore,
> The sinister seduction of the Moon,
> The menace of the irreclaimable Sea.

> Flaunting, tawdry and grim,
> From cloud to cloud along her beat,
> Leering her battered and inveterate leer,
> She signals where he prowls in the dark alone,
> Her horrible old man,
> Mumbling old oaths and warming
> His villainous old bones with villainous talk—

In its broken rhythms and anti-romantic imagery (the moon as
a shabby prostitute) this poem is prophetic of T. S. Eliot and the
nineteen-twenties. One of the great needs of English poetry after
the great Victorians was a new kind of verse free from the intolerable staleness of hackneyed rhymes and the smoothness of traditional rhythms. To create a 'free' verse which would express by its
movement the restlessness and spiritual disintegration of the modern
world and yet would have a satisfying pattern, was a task which
presented problems of immense difficulty, and Henley must be
credited with the distinction of making the first resolute and
intelligent attempt to solve them. His humorous realism, too, in
such poems as 'London Types' helped considerably in breaking
down the pompous and orotund traditions of Victorian literary
verse.

Henley's fine, courageous vision of external realities was not,
unfortunately, matched by a corresponding intellectual and
emotional maturity. The poverty of his inner life is revealed by the
triviality of many of his ballades and rondeaux, and still more by
the blustering imperialism of his political poems and the senseless
swagger of his well-known and much anthologised 'Invictus'. His
patriotic poems suffered from exactly the same kind of hollowness
as Blunt's anti-patriotic poems:

> What have I done for you,
> England, my England?

What is there I would not do,
England, my own?
With your glorious eyes austere,
As the Lord were walking near,
Whispering terrible things and dear
As the song on your bugles blown,
        England—
Round the world on your bugles blown!

This is the shallow rhetoric of the journalist or after-dinner speaker, and the image of a personified England whose eyes are 'glorious' and 'austere', as 'the Lord were walking near' prefigures Kipling's mixture of Old Testament religion with patriotic sentiment of the music-hall variety.

Rudyard Kipling (1865–1936) was the most celebrated of the poets who made the 'voyage without' and by far the most popular English poet of his age. Although he was not thirty-five till the turn of the century, his work was already an important historical fact in the age of the Diamond Jubilee, the Dreyfus Case and the trouble in South Africa. Kipling's character and genius were products of a peculiar combination of circumstances. He was born in India and spent his early childhood and his early manhood there. He had family connections with the Pre-Raphaelites and a connection with the army through his education at a semi-military school. Finally he served his apprenticeship as a writer by working as a journalist in India. Kipling was certainly the greatest English journalist since Dickens, an astonishing observer of facts and manipulator of words. His early verses on Anglo-Indian themes are the work of a supernaturally clever schoolboy, a curious mixture of vers-de-société and parody of Browning and Swinburne. He found himself as a poet on his return from India in 1889 when he lived in Villiers Street above 'the establishment of Harris the Sausage King, who for tuppence gave as much sausage and mash as would carry one from breakfast to dinner', frequented the London pubs and music-halls and listened to 'the observed and compelling songs of the Lion and Mammoth Comiques, and the shriller strains of the Bessies and Bellas'. 'The smoke, the roar, and the good fellowship of relaxed humanity at Gatti's "set" the scheme for a certain type of song'. There Kipling met the English private soldier whom he thought he 'knew fairly well in India', and listened to him with the comments of the barmaid for chorus. This was the period of his most vital poetry, the *Barrack Room*

Ballads and the great poems of seafaring life, capitalism and machinery, such as 'MacAndrew's Hymn', 'The Mary Gloster' and 'The Bolivar'. The models for these poems are not to be found in English 'literary' poetry, but in the popular verse of the day, the songs of the late Victorian music-hall (then at the height of its glory) and the 'recitation pieces' of George R. Sims (author of 'Christmas Day in the Workhouse'). The Kipling of these poems is a great popular ballad-poet, the literary descendant not of Milton, Wordsworth and Keats, but of Elderton, Deloney, D'Urfey, Henry Carey and the Swift of *Mrs Harris's Petition*. While the aesthetes of the Tragic Generation withdrew into their private dreamworlds, Kipling plunged into the noise, the smoke, the slang and the vulgarity of a world of hard bitten engineers, soldiers, sailors and capitalists. He makes his readers not only see and hear, but feel, smell and taste this world.

> I'm 'ere in a ticky ulster an' a broken billycock 'at,
> A-laying on to the sergeant, I don't know a gun from a bat;
> My shirt's doin' duty for jacket, my socks stickin' out o' my boots.
> And I'm learnin' the damned old goose-step along o' the new recruits! [1]
> . . . .
>
> Banged against the iron decks, bilges choked with coal;
> Flayed and frozen foot and hand, sick of heart and soul;
> 'Last we prayed she'd buck herself into Judgment Day
> Hi! we cursed the *Bolivar* knocking round the bay. [2]

His old Scottish fleet engineer MacAndrew is a masterly realistic portrait, the summit of Kipling's achievement, a living man and at the same time the symbol of his age, the early machine age. The identification of the Calvinist system of determinism with the liner's engines is a great stroke of creative imagination. It is one of Kipling's few memorable poetic images, no mere conceit, but a metaphor embodying a profound historical truth, the intimate spiritual connection between Calvinism and modern industrialism:

>   . . . yon orchestra sublime
> Whaurto—uplifted like the Just—the tail-rods mark the time,
> The crank-throws give the double-bass, the feed-pump sobs an ''heaves,
> An' now the main eccentrics start their quarrel on the sheaves:
> Her time, her own appointed time, the rocking link-head bides,

[1] 'Back to the Army Again' (*Barrack Room Ballads*).
[2] 'The Ballad of the Bolivar' (1890).

Till—hear that note?—the rod's return whings glimmering' through
     the guides.
They're all awa'! True beat, full power, the clangin' chorus goes,
Clear to the tunnel where they sit, my purring dynamoes.
Interdependence absolute, foreseen, ordained, decreed, . . .

Kipling's revival of the rough, supple, colloquial verse of the
English popular tradition was a memorable achievement. He
brought a healthy vulgarity back to a poetry which had grown
excessively bookish and refined, but unfortunately he also surrendered
himself completely to the vulgar ethics of the crowd. Like the
typical 'man of action' of his period, he loved facts but hated and
feared reality. All his work is coloured by his denial of the existence
of the fundamental problems of the modern world. There was no
Irish or South African problem, only rebels and traitors; there
was no aesthetic problem, only wasters and rotters like Sir Anthony
Gloster's son who was educated at 'Harrer an' Trinity College'
and 'muddled with books and pictures', and Tomlinson whose sins
were entirely literary; there was no problem of war and peace,
only foolish liberals and sentimental or knavish pacifists. All the
world needed was more discipline, obedience and loyalty, and above
all a paternal British Empire with its unselfish and efficient admin-
istrators and admirable army licked into shape by perfect N.C.O.s.
But Kipling protests too much. He keeps shouting these things so
loudly that it is obvious that he is uneasy. In some of the poems
written during the Boer War this uneasiness even finds expression
in criticism of the very system which he had hymned with an
almost religious esctasy in his earlier writings.

>An' it all went into the laundry,
>But it never came out in the wash.
>We were sugared about by the old men
>(Panicky, perishin' old men)
>That 'amper and 'inder an' scold men
>For fear of Stellenbosch.

Unfortunately he never developed this kind of criticism, and in
the twentieth century he became the poet of the rich and the
great (the 'panicky, perishin' old men'), the laureate of the Carlton
Club and the Morning Post, a sort of medicine man of the upper
middle class, who was always trying to exorcise the spirits of
liberalism, pacifism, bolshevism, and modernism by means of
clanging metallic verses.

Besides the ballad poet and the Imperialist magician, there was a shy and delicate lyrist in Kipling, the creator of the Lama in *Kim* and of the exquisite snatches of song in many of his books and stories:

> They shut the road through the woods
> Seventy years ago.
> Weather and rain have undone it again,
> And now you would never know
> There was once a road through the woods
> Before they planted the trees.
> It is underneath the coppice and heath,
> And the thin anemones.

There was no contact between this Kipling and the loudmouthed Kipling who hymned 'the white man's burden' just as there was no contact between the world of the Lama and that of the players of the 'Great Game'.

Kipling was the boldest adventurer who made the 'voyage without'. He was only too successful as an explorer. He settled among the natives and never returned. He was a considerable poet, but he sacrificed his genius to a soul-destroying creed, which denied the inner life, and led to a worship of brute force, and, ultimately, to the Fascism and Nazism of the nineteen-thirties. Far too honest and humane to be a Fascist, at the end of his life he removed from his books the sign of the swastika to show his disapproval of the Nazi horrors. Nevertheless, it is significant that the books were once decorated with this sign, which was perfectly in harmony with the spirit of such a poem as 'Loot' in *Barrack Room Ballads*.

John Davidson (1857–1909), who began his life as a Glasgow schoolmaster, associated with the Rhymers at the Cheshire Cheese, but his writings bear little resemblance to theirs. He was a bold experimenter in poetic drama, and a lyric poet of considerable power and originality. His blank verse dramas and his later philosophical 'Testaments' written under the influence of Nietzsche, are now literary curiosities, but in some of his lyrics he made the 'voyage without' as successfully as Kipling. In 'Thirty Bob a Week' he actually makes poetry out of the 'uniformity of decent squalor' of which nine-tenths of Victorian urban life was composed.

> For like a mole I journey in the dark,
> A-travelling along the underground

B

From my Pillared Halls and broad Suburbean Park
To come to the daily dull official round;
And home again at night with my pipe all alight,
A-scheming how to count ten-bob a pound.

'Waiting' is a powerful expression of the sense of frustration in a society that condemned some of its best human material to rust unused:

Though lands await our toil,
And earth half empty rolls,
Cumberers of English soil,
We cringe for orts and doles—
Prosperity's accustomed foil,
Millions of useless souls
In the gutters and the ditches,
Human vermin festering lurk—
We the rust upon your riches,
We, the flaw upon your work.

Although Davidson is a much smaller artist than Kipling, he never identified himself with the vulgar morality of the 'man of action' as Kipling did. His long poems tend to be incoherent and shapeless, but his best lyrics contain a penetrating criticism of his age by a bold, original, and truly poetic mind.

2

HARDY AND HOUSMAN

Thomas Hardy (1840–1928) began writing poetry in his early youth, but he made his literary reputation at first as a novelist, and only devoted his energies wholly to poetry after his disappointment with the reception of his last great novel, *Jude the Obscure* (1895). The bulk of his work as a poet was produced in the last thirty years of his long life, and he is, above all, a poet of the crisis that followed the collapse of the Victorian compromise.

He had the good fortune to be born and brought up in a part of England which for long escaped the standardisation of the industrial age and the resulting debasement of human sensibility. The Dorset that he knew in his youth had changed very little for centuries, although in his lifetime he saw it completely transformed. In a letter to Rider Haggard, dated March, 1902, he describes some of the results of that transformation:

For example, if you ask one of the workfolk (they always used to be called 'workfolk' hereabouts . . . 'labourers' is an imported word) the names of surrounding hills, streams, the characters and circumstances of people buried in particular graves; at what spots parish personages lie interred; questions on local fairies, ghosts, herbs, etc., they can give no answer: yet, I recollect the time when the places of burial even of the poor and tombless were all remembered, and the history of the parish and the squire's family for 150 years back known. Such and such ballads appertained to such and such a locality, ghost tales were attached to particular sites, and nooks where wild herbs grew for the cure of divers maladies were pointed out readily.

When Hardy was a boy, he attended one of the last Harvest Homes in Dorset where the old traditional ballads were sung:

the railway having been extended to Dorchester just then, and the orally transmitted ditties of centuries being slain at a stroke by the London comic songs which were introduced. The particular ballad which he remembered hearing that night from the lips of the farmwomen was that one variously called 'The Outlandish Knight', 'May Colvine', 'The Western Tragedy', etc. He could recall to old age the scene of the young women in their light gowns sitting on a bench against the wall in the barn, and leaning against each other, as they warbled the Dorset version of the ballad, which differed a little from the northern:

> Lie there, lie there, thou false hearted man,
>   Lie there instead o' me;
> For six pretty maidens thou hast drowned here,
>   But the seventh hath drown-ed thee!
>   . . . .
> O tell me no more, my pretty par-rot,
>   Lay not the blame on me;
> And your cage shall be made o' the glittering gold,
>   Wi' a door of the white ivo-rie! [1]

This passage from Mrs Hardy's *Early Life of Thomas Hardy* [2] gives a glimpse of a society with a true peasant culture descending from the Middle Ages and remaining intact till the middle of the nineteenth century. It was a world where, as Browning said of the Italians, the people *were* poetry.

Hardy was not a peasant himself; he was the son of a Dorset builder, belonging to a family of small landowners, who had declined into the lower middle class, but who, nevertheless, had traditions of musical and literary culture. He was thus brought up in close contact with the Dorset peasant folk with their rich country lore, their ballads and their love of local history and legends, and at the same time, he was sufficiently removed from them to view them with some detachment. Nevertheless, he is closer to the peasantry and their traditional culture than any English poet since

[1] See *English and Scottish Ballads*, ed. Child-Kittredge, p. 6, for the northern version of this ballad.
[2] Op. cit., pp. 25, 26.

Langland with the single exception of John Clare. He knew the life of the farmer and the field worker at first hand; and he could see the countryside through their eyes, without any of the illusions or sentimentalities of the town-bred observer. His education was a singularly fortunate one for a poet. He went to a good country school where he learned Latin and some French and German. Later, like his own Jude, he taught himself Greek. At home he read the Bible and Shakespeare and learned to play the fiddle, acquiring from his father a knowledge of 'some hundreds of jigs and country dances' as well as much Church music. He left school at the age of sixteen and entered the office of a Dorchester architect as a pupil. With the help of his friend, Horace Moule, Fellow of Queens College, Cambridge, he read Aeschylus and Sophocles in his spare time, while he continued to play his violin with his father and uncle at weddings, christenings and Christmas parties. Thus he acquired a considerable practical knowledge of the arts of architecture and music as well as some classical scholarship without the conventional public school education of the gentry, and at the same time he had unrivalled opportunities of absorbing the richest surviving peasant culture in England.

At the age of twenty-one he went to work in the office of a London architect where he was employed for the next six years. He was an eager and omnivorous reader, and in London he came into contact with the chief currents of contemporary European thought, beginning with John Stuart Mill, Darwin and Huxley, and proceeding later to Comte, Schopenhauer, and Von Hartmann, whose philosophy of the unconscious made a deep impression on him. He escaped from architecture by becoming a successful novelist and from about 1870 till 1897 most of his energies were devoted to the composition of seventeen volumes of prose fiction, the famous series of Wessex novels. Hardy was a novelist belonging to the great Victorian tradition of Dickens, Thackeray, Trollope and George Eliot. He was a great artist in that tradition, using its methods of characterisation and plot construction, but his material was unlike that of his predecessors. His originality as a novelist lies partly in the masterly use which he makes of his knowledge of the rich Wessex peasant life as he knew it in his youth. One of the chief themes of his great novels is the change summarised in the letter to Rider Haggard, quoted at the beginning of this chapter, the transformation of the 'statuesque dynasties' of 'dear delightful Wessex', by the impact of the 'new and strange spirit without, like that which entered the lonely valley of Ezekiel's vision and made the dry bones move'.[1] Hardy was exceedingly sensitive to human suffering and the aspect of the changes in Wessex life that made the strongest impression on him was the tragedy of the Dorset peasant folk whose lives were wrecked by contact with the 'new and strange spirit': the tragedy of Tess, of Giles Winterbourne, of Michael Henchard and of Jude Fawley. In the ruin of such lives he saw also the manifestation of a more universal tragedy arising out of the very existence of human consciousness in a universe apparently controlled by an unconscious power which is entirely indifferent to the aspirations which alone make consciousness endurable. The Wessex novels have more poetry in them than any English novels of the nineteenth century and, with the exception of *Wuthering Heights*, they are the only great tragic novels of the century. This tragic vision is the vision of a poet, and Coventry Patmore showed singular acuteness of judgment when, as early as 1873, he declared that the 'unequalled beauty and power' which he found in *A Pair of Blue Eyes* ought to be expressed in the form of verse. The writing of prose fiction certainly absorbed much of the young Hardy's energy which might have produced notable poetry, but, nevertheless, it provided a magnificent training for a poet. It gave him a knowledge of humanity and a training in dramatic art comparable to that of a writer for the theatre in a great age of poetic drama. His poetry is an entirely separate achievement from his fiction, and it belongs really to the post-Victorian world; nevertheless it owes much to the novels and this debt is by no means confined to poems which deal with characters and situations drawn from them, such as the beautiful verses on Tess and Marty South.

Hardy's earliest known poem 'Domicilium' is a piece of Wordsworthian blank verse probably written before he was twenty, but his first published volume of verse, *Wessex Poems* (1898) contains a number of pieces which were written in the eighteen-sixties and thus belong chronologically to the period of Tennyson's *Enoch Arden*, Swinburne's *Atalanta in Calydon*, and Morris's *Earthly Paradise*. They are strangely unlike any of these works and already exhibit nearly all the chief charactersistics of Hardy's mature poetry. The reader will look in vain in these poems for the rich, sensuous music of the great Victorian poets, who were always trying to follow Keats's advice to 'load every rift with ore' and to surprise with 'a fine excess' of visual beauty and melody. Hardy's aim was

---

[1] See *A Group of Noble Dames* (1896), 'The First Countess of Wessex'.

quite different; like Browning, the only Victorian poet by whom he was strongly influenced, and Donne, whose work he greatly admired, he was trying to produce a dramatic rather than a pictorial or musical effect. He differed from Browning, however, in avoiding the romantic and the picturesque, and in his deliberate use of commonplace and contemporary subject matter. In one of his notes he praises a painter for infusing 'emotion into the baldest external objects':

'This accords with my feeling about say Heidelberg and Baden *versus* Scheveningen—as I wrote at the beginning of the *Return of the Native*—that the beauty of association is entirely superior to the beauty of aspect . . . paradoxically put, it is to see beauty in ugliness'. A great deal of Hardy's poetry arises out of his perception of 'beauty in ugliness'. It is important to notice that Hardy never advocated a cult of ugliness for its own sake. He rather sought to extend the boundaries of poetic sensibility by an expression of new types of beauty and significance which he found in the ugly and the commonplace. 'I think', he writes in a diary kept in 1877, 'the art lies in making these defects . . . the basis of a hitherto unperceived beauty, by irradiating them with the 'light that never was' on their surface, but is to be seen latent in them by the spiritual eye'.

Wessex Poems are certainly the work of a writer who has made the 'voyage without' into the world of action and the life of common men. The early ballad poems in dialect such as 'The Bride Night Fire' (1866) and 'Valenciennes' (1878) are renderings in verse of the same sort of material that he used in his prose fiction, the common humanity of the Wessex village with its rustic humour and pathos and its rustic clumsiness and uncouthness seen through the eyes of an entirely unsentimental observer.

The poet of 'The Bride Night Fire' might have become a sort of Wessex Kipling, a writer of vigorous, homely ballads full of the tang of peasant life. There is no doubt that in these early poems, Hardy owed much to the example of the Rev. William Barnes (1800–1886) the Dorset dialect poet, whose work he greatly admired. Barnes was a curious mixture of a Wessex dialect poet of peasant life and a learned philologist with a delight in exotic metrical forms which he borrowed from Persian and Welsh poetry. Hardy was never a scholarly metrist like Barnes, but he learned much from Barnes's experiments and he found in Barnes's poetry new verse forms which helped him to avoid the staleness of nineteenth-century academic prosody. In 'The Bride Night Fire' and a few other early poems, Hardy used Dorset dialect freely in the manner of Barnes, but in his more mature work, he only uses an occasional striking or expressive dialect word to relieve the flatness of modern standard English.

It is clear, however, that the author of *Wessex Poems* is neither a Wessex Kipling nor a second Barnes. He has made the 'voyage within' as well as the 'voyage without', and he is an adventurer in the world of the spirit as well as among the homespun realities of the village folk of Wessex. He has a clear perception of the 'schism in the soul' of modern humanity and the courage and honesty to give it a central place in his poetry. One of the most significant of the Wessex poems is 'Neutral Tones', the first of his great tragic lyrics:

> We stood by a pond that winter day,
> And the sun was white, as though chidden of God,
> And a few leaves lay on the starving sod;
>   They were fallen from an ash, and were gray.
>
> Your eyes on me were as eyes that rove
> Over tedious riddles solved years ago;
> And some words played between us to and fro
>   On which lost the more by our love.
>
> The smile on your mouth was the deadest thing
> Alive enough to have strength to die;
> And a grin of bitterness swept thereby
>   Like an ominous bird a-wing. . . .
>
> Since then, keen lessons that love deceives,
> And wings with wrong, have shaped to me
> Your face, and the God-cursed sun, and a tree,
>   And a pond edged with grayish leaves.

This poem and similar ones written by Hardy in later years appear to grow out of a crisis in his own life which probably occurred when he was in the thirties. This crisis seems to have destroyed his youthful buoyancy and idealism, but at the same time to have released remarkable powers of tragic and ironic vision. The 'schism in the soul' is symbolised in this and a number of later poems by the image of a lover's quarrel which has a universal significance reaching far beyond the experience of any individual lovers and revealing a profound and sinister division in the human personality which has lost its old integration with the decay of traditional beliefs. By making this division explicit and showing it in the light of tragedy, Hardy provides the *katharsis* which is a necessary prelude to a new integration.

Another kind of spiritual exploration is seen in the poem called
'Nature's Questioning' where the poet one 'dawning' looks at
'Field, flock and tree' and imagines them saying—

'We wonder, ever wonder, why we find us here!

     'Has some Vast Imbecility,
     Mighty to build and blend,
     But impotent to tend,
Framed us in jest, and left us now to hazardry?

'Or come we of an Automaton
     Unconscious of our pains? . . .
     Or are we live remains
Of Godhead dying downwards, brain and eye now gone?

'Or is it that some high Plan betides
     As yet not understood,
     Of Evil stormed by Good,
We the Forlorn Hope over which Achievement strides?'

This poem is perhaps a little topheavy because the vastness of
the speculations contained in the lines quoted above are rather out
of keeping with the simple natural objects which are supposed to
utter them. Nevertheless it is a very significant achievement. It
gives poetic shape to philosophic speculations which have been
conceived, not only intellectually, but also imaginatively by the
poet. In such work, Hardy to some extent reversed the process of
'dissociation' of intellect and imagination which modern critics
have traced to the mid-seventeenth century, and produced a new
integration of sensibility. He is also giving imaginative expression
for the first time to the kind of consciousness which had been
produced by the scientific discoveries of the nineteenth century.
Swinburne had already attempted to do this in such poems as
'Hertha' and the 'Hymn of Man', but these poems express only a
somewhat naive exultation at the release of the human mind from
ancient superstitions. Hardy shows us what the mind is like when
it has been 'released', its sense of bewilderment and isolation when
confronted by a world picture from which not only God and the
angels but also the immanent divine spirit of the pantheistic romantics has been banished.

From *Wessex Poems* Hardy passed on to a long series of volumes
published between 1897 and 1928 in which he steadily developed

the types of poetry that appeared in his first collection: the realistic, often grotesque ballad, the dramatic lyric, usually tragic or ironic and the poem of cosmic contemplation. In these volumes Hardy treats nearly all the significant aspects of the modern crisis, the relationship between the sexes, the relationship between man and the animals, imperialism and war, the social question and the religious question. Underlying his treatment of all these themes is his tragic conception of the universe. Here he owed much probably to Schopenhauer and Von Hartmann, but the reading of the works of these philosophers only helped him to formulate views which arose from the nature of his own genius. The tragedy for Hardy lies in the contrast between the aspirations of mankind, or even of the animals, and the unconscious cosmic will which controls the universe and is entirely oblivious to moral values. The hopelessness of the struggle against the unconscious will give a tragic grandeur to the sufferings of the humblest creatures. Hardy has a quarrel with official Christianity and he has a quarrel with society, but these quarrels are as nothing as compared with his quarrel with the universe. Like Ivan Karamazov in Dostoevsky's novel, he could not accept the universe as long as it involved the sufferings of a single child (or, Hardy would have added, a single animal). The poems in which he attempts to deal with the cosmic tragedy directly are not very happy because of the inadequacy of his mythology. The figures of the dead God and the shadowy mourners in 'God's Funeral', and of the 'doomsters and spinners of the years,' which recur in several poems, are too obviously constructed for allegorical purposes to be poetically effective and the works in which they occur are impressive in spite of them rather than because of them. The poems which express most completely his tragic view of the universe are those in which he contemplates concrete instances of the universal tragedy such as the solemn and touching lines 'To an Unborn Pauper Child':

> Had I the ear of wombèd souls
> Ere their terrestial chart unrolls,
>   And thou wert free
>   To cease, or be,
>   Then would I tell thee all I know,
> And put it to thee: Wilt thou take Life so?
>
> Vain vow! No hint of mine may hence
> To theeward fly: to thy locked sense

Explain none can
Life's pending plan:
Thou wilt thy ignorant entry make
Though skies spout fire and blood and nations quake.

Fain would I, dear, find some shut plot
Of earth's wide wold for thee, where not
One tear, one qualm,
Should break the calm.
But I am weak as thou and bare;
No man can change the common lot to rare.

Hardy's treatment of the theme of war is remarkable. He wrote groups of poems dealing with the Boer War and the First World War in which he neither denounces imperialism like Blunt, nor exalts militarism like Henley and Kipling. His method is always to show the results of the impact of war on concrete individual human beings like Hodge, the ignorant Wessex drummer, who died in South Africa for a cause which he did not understand and beneath stars that he could not name:

They throw in Drummer Hodge, to rest
Uncoffined—just as found:
His landmark is a kopje-crest
That breaks the veldt around:
And foreign constellations west
Each night above his mound.

Young Hodge the Drummer never knew—
Fresh from his Wessex home—
The meaning of the broad Karoo,
The Bush, the dusty loam,
And why uprose to nightly view
Strange stars amid the gloam.

Yet portion of that unknown plain
Will Hodge for ever be;
His homely Northern breast and brain
Grow to some Southern tree,
And strange-eyed constellations reign
His stars eternally.

The strength of this poem lies in its combination of deep feeling with restraint and dignified simplicity. Far more effectively than any impassioned comment it embodies the tragedy of the destruction of human lives by the vast inhuman mechanism of modern warfare. It arises out of a war which was a mere skirmish compared with the vast struggles that were to follow in the twentieth century, but in it Hardy has already grasped and expressed with prophetic insight the true significance of modern warfare, which was only rediscovered by the 'Trench Poets' of 1917–1918. Indeed one of the most remarkable features of the poetry written by Hardy in the early years of the twentieth century is its prophetic quality. It is haunted by images of death and war and by premonitions of catastrophe expressed in such poems as 'The Convergence of the Twain' (1912) and 'Channel Firing' (April, 1914). 'The Convergence of the Twain', a poem on the loss of the Titanic, is one of Hardy's most impressive achievements:

> In a solitude of the sea
> Deep from human vanity,
> And Pride of Life that planned her, stilly couches she.

> Steel chambers, late the pyres
> Of her salamandrine fires,
> Cold currents thrid, and turn to rhythmic tidal lyres.

> Over the mirrors meant
> To glass the opulent
> The sea-worm crawls—grotesque, slimed, dumb, indifferent.

> Jewels in joy designed
> To ravish the sensuous mind
> Lie lightless, all their sparkles bleared and black and blind.

> Dim moon-eyed fishes near
> Gaze at the gilded gear
> And query: 'What does this vaingloriousness down here?'

> Well: while was fashioning
> This creature of cleaving wing,
> The Immanent Will that stirs and urges everything

> Prepared a sinister mate
> For her—so gaily great—
> A Shape of Ice, for the time far and dissociate!

> And as the smart ship grew
> In stature, grace, and hue,
> In shadowy silent distance grew the Iceberg too. . . .

This noble poem is a study of the tragic theme of cosmic impiety and the nemesis that overtakes it. Hardy utters no word of blame or criticism but the phrases used in connection with the great liner, 'Pride of Life', 'to glass the opulent', 'the sensuous mind', 'gilded gear', 'the smart ship', convey a sense of insolence and shallowness of the civilisation that produced her. The image of the iceberg which destroyed her as 'a sinister mate', prepared for that purpose by the 'Immanent Will', is one of Hardy's supreme poetic creations, a wonderfully effective symbol of the vengeance of nature on a society which has defied her laws.

Hardy's tenderness and compassion extend not only to human beings but to animals, and he is, perhaps, the first great European poet to treat animals with exactly the same respect as human beings. Even the insects such as the 'long legs, moth and dumbledore' with the 'sleepy fly' in the vivid and playful poem called 'An August Midnight' are shown as the poet's honoured guests:

> Thus meet we five, in this still place,
> At this point of time, at this point of space.
> —My guests besmear my new-penned line,
> Or bang at the lamp and fall supine.
> 'God's humblest, they!' I muse. Yet why?
> They know Earth-secrets that know not I.

As Dr Chakravarty has pointed out, Hardy 'had so completely assimilated the theory of evolution and harmonised it with an increase of sensibility that he based thereupon the conception of morality itself not only in relation to man but to the entire world of conscious sentient beings'.[1]

The indignant and intensely pathetic poem called 'The Blinded Bird' is a terrible indictment of a civilization that claims to be Christian. By putting the words of St Paul into the mouth of a blinded singing bird he makes a passionate claim for the application of Christian ethics to man's relationship to animals:

> Who hath charity? this bird
> Who suffereth long and is kind,
> And is not provoked, though blind
> And alive ensepulchred?
> Who hopeth, endureth all things?
> Who thinketh no evil, but sings?
> Who is divine? this bird.

[1] Chakravarty: *The Dynasts and the Post-War Age in Poetry*, p. 23.

Hardy's imaginative apprehension of the kinship of man to the lower animals is a contribution to the growth of human sensibility comparable with the concept of the brotherhood of man which was the great legacy of the romantic poets.

Hardy's chief protection against the pain caused by his sensitiveness to suffering was his gift of irony. He was the first great ironist in English poetry since Pope and Swift. His irony arises from the bitter humour which perceived in the contrast between human hopes and idealisms and the actualities of life. The fierce and ruthless mockery of the famous series of poems called *Satires of Circumstance* (1911), like the satire of Swift, really arises from a profound tenderness and compassion. He uses this kind of mockery as Swift used it to deal with situations which are at once too pathetic and too absurd to be treated naturally or emotionally, as in the poem on the mothers in the cemetery quarrelling over their children's graves:

'You see those mothers squabbling there?'
Remarks the man of the cemetery.
'One says in tears, "'*tis mine lies here!*"
Another, "*Nay, mine, you Pharisee!*"
Another, "*How dare you move my flowers
And put your own on this grave of ours!*"
But all their children were laid therin
At different times, like sprats in a tin.

'And then the main drain had to cross,
And we moved the lot some nights ago,
And packed them away in the general foss
With hundreds more. But their folk don't know,
And as well cry over a new-laid drain
As anything else, to ease your pain!'

The image of the mothers with their loud-mouthed egoism quarrelling over the empty graves is a memorable symbol of the futility of a world that allows itself to be blinded by cheap sentiment in the face of unpleasant realities. Hardy is, however, by no means always a tragic or ironic poet. He is capable of unexpected lightness and delicacy and an enjoyment of simple beauty and charm especially of womanhood, of landscape and of weather; such moods he expressed in poems which obviously owe much to the numerous old 'jigs and country dances' which he learned to play in his youth:

This is the weather the cuckoo likes,
    And so do I;
When showers betumble the chestnut spikes,
    And nestlings fly:
And the little brown nightingale bills his best,
And they sit outside at 'The Travellers' Rest',
And maids come forth sprig-muslin drest
And citizens dream of the south and west,
    And so do I.

Poems like these have the grace and charm of the old English dance music combined with the wholesome solidity and realism which is derived from the folk culture which Hardy absorbed in his youth. They belong to the popular tradition of English poetry and have none of the abstract and dreamlike quality of the English poetry in the learned Apollonian tradition. In place of Keats's Cynthia or the romantic damsels of Tennyson and Rossetti, Hardy gives us Lizbie Browne:

Dear Lizbie Browne
Where are you now?
In sun, in rain?—
Or is your brow
Past joy, past pain,
Dear Lizbie Browne?

Sweet Lizbie Browne
How you could smile,
How you could sing!—
How archly wile
In glance giving
Sweet Lizbie Browne!

And, Lizbie Browne
Who else had hair
Bay-red as yours,
Or flesh so fair
Bred out of doors,
Sweet Lizbie Browne?

He uses these dance rhythms very successfully to express a tender wistfulness in a notable group of poems which apparently refer to his memories of his first wife, such as 'The Voice':

Woman much missed, how you call to me, call to me,
Saying that now you are not as you were
When you had changed from the one that was all to me,
But as at first when our day was fair.

Can it be you that I hear? Let me view you then,
Standing as when I drew near to the town
Where you would wait for me: yes as I knew you then,
Even to the original air-blue gown!

Or is it only the breeze, in its listlessness
Travelling across the wet mead to me here,
You being ever dissolved to existlessness,
Heard no more again far or near?

Thus I; faltering forward,
Leaves around me falling,
Wind oozing thin through the thorn from norward
And the woman calling.

We see the ghostly figure of a woman moving to the rhythm of the dance, which becomes fainter and fainter, as she recedes into the distance and fades into 'existlessness'. Then, as she disappears, the abrupt change of the metre in the last stanza reveals a close-up view of the forlorn figure of a man plodding through an autumnal landscape.

Hardy excels in poems like this, wonderfully sensitive records of moments of consciousness. 'Unadjusted impressions', he wrote in his preface to his second volume of verse, 'have their value and the road to a true philosophy of life seems to lie in humbly recording diverse readings of its phenomena as they are forced upon us by chance or change'. This statement can be compared with the words of Walter Pater: 'Not the fruit of experience, but experience itself, is the end'.[1] Hardy recreated for his own age that type of poem in which the centre of interest is not to be found in external objects, but in the poet's own consciousness. This is one of his most important legacies to twentieth-century poets, for it is a means by which the poet can effectively subdue and transmute the ordinariness and drabness of modern life. Thus in the poem called 'Beyond the Last Lamp', Hardy recalls a couple whom he saw walking slowly in a lane at Tooting one wet night. He knew nothing of the couple and the sight was a perfectly ordinary one, but thirty years later he could not think of the 'lone lane' without calling up the vision of the 'mysterious tragic pair'.

Though thirty years of blur and blot
Have slid since I beheld that spot,

[1] W. Pater, *The Renaissance* (ed. 1928), p. 249.

> And saw in curious converse there
> > Moving slowly, moving sadly
> > That mysterious tragic pair,
> Its olden look may linger on—
> All but the couple; they have gone.
>
> Whither? Who knows indeed . . . and yet
> To me, when nights are weird and wet,
> Without these comrades there at tryst
> > Creeping slowly, creeping sadly,
> > That lone lane does not exist.
> There they seem brooding on their pain,
> And will, while such a lane remain.

Such a poem achieves a true synthesis of the inner and the outer lives. An apparently commonplace event, when it is mirrored in the poet's consciousness, assumes a quality of mysterious beauty and strangeness. The typically modern self-consciousness can thus be used to create a new sort of poetic material and to achieve, in Hardy's own phrase, a true 'exploration of reality'.

The same method was used by Hardy on a vast scale in his great epic drama *The Dynasts* (1903–1908). He had a good deal of the mentality of the scientific historian or antiquary. In his boyhood, his interest had been aroused by records of the preparations in Dorset for the threatened invasion in the time of Napoleon, and since then he had made an elaborate and careful study of the historical records of the Napoleonic Wars. At one time, he thought of using the results of this study for a series of epic ballads with Napoleon 'as a sort of Achilles'. He abandoned this plan, however, in favour of an immense chronicle play, a long series of scenes in blank verse and prose depicting the most significant aspects of the great European conflict from Trafalgar to Waterloo. In choosing this subject for his most ambitious work, Hardy showed an insight as profound as that of Milton when he chose the story of the Fall as the subject of his epic. History is a form of intellectual activity which is as characteristic of the twentieth century as theology was of the seventeenth. *The Dynasts* is a remarkable achievement merely as a huge chronicle play. The verse rarely rises to any great poetic heights, but the imaginative presentation of historic material is masterly, and such passages as the death of Nelson, the battle of Austerlitz, the vivid picture of the deserters from Sir John Moore's army in the cellar near Astorga and the rustic humour of the Wessex scenes are permanent additions to English dramatic poetry. *The Dynasts*, however, is something far greater and more significant than a chronicle play. The poet unifies the whole vast historical pageant by enclosing it in another drama which takes place in a remote region far above the earth. The actors in this supernatural drama are spirits who watch the human drama from their exalted station, sometimes coming close to it and even occasionally mingling with the human actors. These superhuman characters are not conceived as having an objective existence, but, as Hardy writes in his preface, are presented as 'contrivances of the fancy merely'. Actually, they are embodiments of the chief elements in the typical modern mind so that the whole drama is seen mirrored in the consciousness of a representative spectator.

There are numerous groups of spirits, but the most significant are the Spirit of the Years who represents complete intellectual and scientific impartiality, the Pities who speak for the compassionate and humanitarian element in the modern mind and the Ironies who are the voice of that very characteristic modern spirit which takes a perverse delight in the contrasts between brutal actualities and moral values.

The Spirit of the Years, like a good-humoured old gentleman, consents to sit out a few acts of the play and interpret it to the other spirits. He shows them the whole human drama as the work of an 'Immanent Will' which controls all phenomena working unconsciously in a sort of trance. This conception of a vast unconscious Will completes Hardy's masterly portrayal of the structure of the modern mind. His interest in Von Hartmann's theory of the unconscious has already been mentioned. Long before the twentieth-century writers who were influenced by Freud and the Viennese school of psychology, he not only realized the importance of the conception of the unconscious, but used it effectively for literary purposes:

> In that immense unweeting Mind is shown
> One far above forethinking; purposive,
> Yet superconscious; a Clairvoyancy
> That knows not what It knows, yet works therewith.
> . . . .
> So the Will heaves through Space, and moulds the times,
> With Mortals for Its fingers! We shall see
> Again men's passions, virtues, visions, crimes,
>   Obey resistlessly
> The purposive, unmotived, dominant Thing
> Which sways in brooding dark their wayfaring!

It is to be noted that, unlike some later writers, Hardy never made an idol of the unconscious, or saw in surrender to it a means of salvation for humanity. Indeed, speaking through the mouths of the Pities, he lamented its blindness and in the famous concluding chorus suggested that the one hope for the world was that the Will would one day awake to complete consciousness:

Consciousness the Will informing, till It fashion all things fair!

The supernatural drama in *The Dynasts* is an imaginative invention of the first order. It enables the reader to see the historical pageant from a position where the movements of great masses of humanity are visible.[1] Some critics have complained that *The Dynasts* contains no great heroic figures like those of Greek or Elizabethan drama. *The Dynasts*, however, belongs to an age of collectivism and its true hero is not Nelson or Napoleon but the inarticulate suffering masses of Europe. Nowhere does Hardy show himself to be more truly a representative of this age than in his power of visualising great mass movements of humanity. This power is magnificently exercised in the stage directions of *The Dynasts*, which, though in prose, are an essential part of Hardy's poetry:

> *The point of view then sinks downwards through space, and draws near to the surface of the perturbed countries, where the peoples, distressed by events which they did not cause, are seen writhing, crawling, heaving, and vibrating in their various cities and nationalities.*
> . . . .
> *The silent insect creep of the Austrian columns towards the banks of the Inn continues to be seen till the view fades into nebulousness and dissolves.*
> . . . .
> *The caterpillar shape still creeps laboriously nearer, but instead of increasing in size by the rules of perspective, it gets more attenuated, and there are left upon the ground behind it minute parts of itself, which are speedily flaked over, and remain as white pimples by the wayside.*

In *The Dynasts* Hardy created a great myth out of the typically modern intellectual activities of history and psychology. Here as in many of his shorter poems, he succeeded, in a sense, in overcoming the modern crisis by making it explicit and giving poetic form

[1] In his power of shifting the focus of his great panoramic view and his masterly use of the close-up, Hardy anticipates the art of the film director. It is surprising that no attempt has been made to make a film of *The Dynasts*.

to a tragic vision of life reflected in the modern consciousness. His achievement was, perhaps, only possible for one who had the rare opportunity of uniting to a sensibility produced by a rich peasant culture an apprehension of the most significant currents of modern European thought. Nevertheless, his poetry is pregnant with suggestions for the future and already it may be seen as occupying a position at the opening of the twentieth century as significant as that of Wordsworth at the opening of the nineteenth.

Alfred Edward Housman (1859–1936) is a much smaller poet than Hardy, whom he resembles superficially in several respects. Born and brought up in Worcestershire (not Shropshire), he was the son of a solicitor and a member of a gifted family with a facilty for the writing of verse. He obtained a first class in Classical Moderations at Oxford, but failed in his Final Examination in 'Greats'. After a period during which he worked as a clerk in the Patent Office, he was appointed Professor of Latin in University College, London. From London, he passed to Cambridge in 1911, when he became Professor of Latin in that University and a Fellow of Trinity College. He achieved an international reputation as a classical scholar, famous alike for his erudition and the caustic satire of his polemics against other scholars. Only two small volumes of his verse were published during his lifetime. The first was the celebrated Shropshire Lad (1895); the second appeared after an interval of a quarter of a century in 1922. A third collection of about the same size as the other two was published after his death by his brother, the poet and dramatist, Laurence Housman, whose memoir of A. E. Housman includes a few additional poems.

Housman's Shropshire, like Hardy's Wessex, is a part of England full of historic memories and still comparatively free from the taint of industrialism, but, unlike Hardy, Housman had no real contact with a traditional popular culture. He himself admitted that he 'never spent much time there', but he made some exquisite poetry out of his appreciation of its landscape and used about twenty of its place names very effectively. Out of his memories of the west country, he constructed a curious dreamworld (well described by R. M. Hewitt as an 'inverted Arcadia') in which Shropshire Lads drink beer, play football, commit murders, enlist in red-coated Victorian regiments, and either die in outposts of the empire or are hanged in Ludlow Gaol. This pseudo-pastoral fantasy seems partly to conceal and partly to symbolise a profound emotional disturbance in the poet's life of which nothing is known. As C. M. Bowra has written, it is 'unable to carry the weight of the fearful events which are assumed to take place'. Housman certainly made the 'voyage within' but he was too prim and fastidious to give more than some cryptic hints of what he found there. His 'voyage without' was rather in the nature of a scholar's daydream of rustic virility and violence than a genuine exploration. Nevertheless, in a few poems he gave powerful expression to the division in the modern consciousness caused by the contrasts between the development of the moral sense (Hardy's 'Pities' in *The Dynasts*) and the dehumanised world-picture provided by the discoveries of the scientists. In one of the best of his poems suggested by his Shropshire memories, he finds an effective image for this spiritual division in the tradition of the wars between Saxon and Celt on the Welsh Marches:

> In my heart it has not died,
> The war that sleeps on Severn side;
> They cease not fighting, east and west,
> On the marches of my breast.
>
> Here the truceless armies yet
> Trample, rolled in blood and sweat,
> They kill and kill and never die;
> And I think that each is I.
>
> None will part us, none undo
> The knot that makes one flesh of two,
> Sick with hatred, sick with pain,
> Strangling—When shall we be slain?

In one poem, founded apparently on a hint from Baudelaire, he achieves tragic dignity in the direct treatment of this theme:

> Be still, my soul, be still; the arms you bear are brittle,
>   Earth and high Heaven are fixt of old and founded strong.
> Think rather—call to thought, if now you grieve a little,
>   The days when we had rest, O soul, for they were long.
>
> Men loved unkindness then, but lightless in the quarry
>   I slept and saw not; tears fell down, I did not mourn;
> Sweat ran and blood sprang out and I was never sorry:
>   Then it was well with me, in days ere I was born.

It is only, however, in a few personal utterances like this, that Housman makes a significant contribution to the poetry of the modern crisis. His treatment of the subject of war can be contrasted with Hardy's. Hardy's poem on 'Drummer Hodge' (see p. 41) is a profound comment on the meaning of modern warfare. Housman's poems on soldiers like 'Lancer' recall the sentimental oleographs which adorned the walls of late Victorian kitchens and nurseries:

> I 'listed at home for a lancer,
>> *O who would not sleep with the brave?*
> I 'listed at home for a lancer
>> To ride on a horse to my grave.
>
> And over the seas we were bidden
>> A country to take and to keep;
> And far with the brave I have ridden,
>> And now with the brave I shall sleep.

Even his famous 'Epitaph on an Army of Mercenaries' is rather a superb piece of versified rhetoric than a moving poem.

Housman might have been a great poet of the modern crisis, but he was inhibited by a certain primness and reticence, and his mind never developed beyond the defiant atheism of a Victorian adolescent. A few of his later poems such as 'Her strong enchantments failing' (*Last Poems*, no. III), and the sombre and impressive 'Hell Gate' (*Last Poems*, no. XXXI) suggest that he might have found in traditional mythologies more successful symbols than the incredible peasants and soldiers of *A Shropshire Lad*.

THE POLYTECHNIC OF WALES.
LIBRARY
TREFOREST

3

HOPKINS AND BRIDGES

'The accepted notion of a poet would appear to be a sort of male odalisque, singing or piano-playing a kind of spiced ideas, second-hand reminiscence, or toying late hours at entertainments in rooms stifling with fashionable scent.' These words were written by Walt Whitman (1819-1888), the American poet, who made a determined and memorable effort to free poetry from the tameness, the preciousness and the backward-looking antiquarianism which tended to turn it into a pleasant parlour game both in England and America in the second half of the nineteenth century. Whitman tried to create for the modern democratic world a new poetry, freed from all the trammels of the feudal, aristocratic past, in order to express the life of the masses in the teeming cities of the young United States. As he was a poet of genius with a natural gift for sinewy rhythmical eloqence, he had a considerable measure of success. He abandoned rhyme and traditional metre, and thought he had created an entirely new poetic form. Actually he was influenced by tradition far more than he imagined, and his long, irregular, unrhymed lines echo the rhythm of Longfellow's accentual hexameters, Carlyle's rhapsodies, Ossian-Macpherson's prose poems and the majestic music of the Jacobean English Bible. Whitman, nevertheless, brought back into poetry the energy and the savagery of the natural man, which had been banished from it by ages of courtly refinement and gentlemanly tradition. He flung himself with all the ardour of his energetic nature into the expression of the richness of his healthy, uninhibited vision of the external world:

Smile O voluptuous cool-breath'd earth!
Earth of the slumbering and liquid trees!
Earth of departed sunset—earth of the mountains misty-topt!
Earth of the vitreous pour of the moon just tinged with blue!
Earth of shine and dark mottling the tide of the river!
Earth of the limpid gray, of clouds brighter and clearer for my sake!
Far-swooping elbow'd earth—rich apple-blossom'd earth!
Smile, for your lover comes
. . . .

I am not the poet of goodness only, I do not decline to be the poet
    of wickedness also.

What blurt is this about virtue and about vice?
Evil propels me and reform of evil propels me, I stand indifferent.
My gait is no fault-finder's or rejecter's gait,
I moisten the roots of all that has grown.

'His poetic genius', writes Santayana of Whitman, 'fell back to
the lowest level, perhaps to which it is possible for poetic genius to
fall. He reduced his imagination to a passive sensorium for the
registering of impressions. No element of construction remained in
it, and therefore no element of penetration. But his scope was wide;
and his lazy desultory apprehension was poetical'.

The strength of Whitman lies in his courage, his simplicity, his
universality and his healthy, life-giving joy in the whole variegated
pageant of animate and inanimate things. His irregular unrhymed
rhythms are too loose and too undisciplined to be a suitable instru-
ment for great poetic art, but they are full of suggestions for a new
prosody descending from the large free rhythms of English poetic
prose. His weakness lies in his barbaric and uncultivated personality
and his spiritual emptiness. He is one of the revolutionists of whom
Santayana wrote that it is their misfortune 'that they are disinherited,
and their folly is that they wish to be more disinherited than they
are. Hence in the midst of their passionate and even heroic idealisms,
there is commonly a strange poverty in their minds . . . and an
ostentatious vileness in their manners'. It is significant that one of
Whitman's most characteristic poems is called 'The Song of
Myself'. Although he thinks himself free, he is actually (except when
exalted by a great theme as in his funeral ode on Lincoln) enslaved by
his own anarchic and limited personality, and the result is that much
of his poetry is, as he himself put it, 'a mere barbaric yawp'.

Gerard Manley Hopkins (1844–1889) in a letter to his friend
Robert Bridges, dated 1882, wrote: 'I know in my heart Walt
Whitman's mind to be more like my own than any man's living.

As he is a very great scoundrel, this is not a very pleasant confession'. When Hopkins wrote this letter, he was a Jesuit priest and he was also a Victorian English gentleman. By calling Whitman 'a very great scoundrel', he probably means that he was not a Christian and that his ethical standards were not those of the English Victorian upper middle class. It is, nevertheless, remarkable that he recognized a profound kinship between Walt Whitman's mind and his own. He felt a deep, instinctive sympathy with Whitman's barbaric energy, his uninhibited sensuality and his revolt against a tame and enervating civilisation.

Hopkins was one of the most gifted Englishmen of his generation. He came from a middle class family of professional people with strong artistic interests. He went up to Oxford as a scholar of Balliol in 1863. There he was a pupil of Walter Pater and made a great impression on Benjamin Jowett, then Regius Professor of Greek, who called him 'the star of Balliol'. Among his friends was a young Etonian called Robert Bridges who was already intensely interested in poetic craftsmanship. At Oxford Hopkins wrote some remarkable verse and prose including a masterly philosophic dialogue on Beauty. He won a first class in Greats in 1867 and a brilliant career as a writer and scholar seemed to be open to him. There was, however, a deeply religious strain in his character that prevented him from seizing the worldly success which appeared to be in his grasp. When he came to Oxford, he was an ardent Anglo-Catholic and the influence of the Broad Churchman Jowett and the aesthetic philosopher Pater weighed less with him than the example and prestige of John Henry Newman, who had left Oxford to become a Roman Catholic priest eighteen years before Hopkins matriculated. In 1866 he was received into the Roman Church by Newman at Birmingham, and to the dismay of his parents and friends he became a Jesuit priest, submitting himself wholeheartedly to the rigorous discipline of his Order and not only relinquishing all prospects of a worldly career, but even abandoning his literary work and burning most of his early poetry. For seven years he wrote no verse (except a few trifles), but devoted the whole of his energies to the tasks imposed on him by his superiors. Besides carrying out the arduous system of training imposed on Jesuit novices, he performed parochial duties and taught at Catholic schools.

In 1875 at the suggestion of one of his ecclesiastical superiors, he composed an ode on the wreck of the *Deutschland*, a German ship which had foundered in a snowstorm off the Kentish coast with

five nuns on board who were exiled from Prussia under the Flack
Laws. He sent the manuscript of this ode to Bridges, with whom
he continued to correspond, though Bridges had no sympathy
with his religious views. The ode was in a new metrical form which
Hopkins had been meditating for some time. 'I had long had
haunting my ear the echo of a new rhythm which now I realised
on paper.'[1] Bridges was at first astonished and repelled by the
Deutschland ode, and the Jesuit journal called *The Month*, to which
Hopkins had sent it, refused to publish it. He continued to write
poetry in the new manner and to send his poems to his friends,
Robert Bridges and Canon R. W. Dixon with whom he cor-
responded regularly. Dixon was anxious to arrange for the publication of some of his poems and, at his suggestion, Hopkins sent
three of his sonnets to Hall Caine who was editing an anthology
called *Sonnets of Three Centuries*. Hall Caine refused to print the
sonnets after consulting 'a critic of the highest eminence'. This
incident is a remarkable example of the stubborn conservatism of
English critical opinion in the later nineteenth century. The most
enterprising and original poet of his generation was thus prevented
by it from reaching any public in his lifetime beyond the few
friends who read his poems in manuscript.

After teaching at catholic schools and carrying out parochial
duties in Wales, Liverpool and Glasgow, Hopkins was appointed
in 1884 to the Chair of Classics in the newly founded University
College of Dublin. There he was lonely, overworked and unhappy,
and there he wrote his last poems, the 'terrible sonnets'. He died of
typhoid in Dublin in 1889. Most of his papers passed into the hands
of Robert Bridges who published a few of the poems with a short
memoir in 1893 in A. H. Miles's *Poets and Poetry of the Nineteenth
Century*. The first collected edition, edited by Bridges with Hopkin's
own introduction and notes, did not appear till 1918.

In an early poem called 'A Vision of the Mermaids', written while
he was still at school, Hopkins shows a richness of sensuous imagination akin to that of young Keats and, although the form is traditional, comparable with that of Whitman:

> Soon—as when Summer of his sister Spring
> Crushes and tears the rich enjewelling,
> And boasting 'I have fairer things than these'
> Plashes amidst the billowy apple-trees
> His lusty hands, in gusts of scented wind

---

[1] Letter to R. W. Dixon, October, 1878 (*Letters*, Ed. Abbott II 14).

> Swirling out bloom till all the air is blind
> With rosy foam and pelting blossom and mists
> Of driving vermeil-rain. . . .

The young Hopkins, however, seems to have been impressed not only by the sensuous richness of the world as he saw it, but also by its spiritual emptiness. A remarkable poem written at Oxford in the style of Matthew Arnold, contains a vision of a universe from which spirit has been banished:

> God, though to Thee our psalm we raise,
> No answering voice comes from the skies;
> To Thee the trembling sinner prays
> But no forgiving voice replies;
> Our prayer seems lost in desert ways,
> Our hymn in the vast silence dies.

> We see the glories of the earth
> But not the hand that wrought them all:
> Night to a myriad worlds gives birth,
> Yet like a lighted empty hall
> Where stands no host at door or hearth
> Vacant creation's lamps appal.

This undergraduate had already made the 'voyage without' but he had the intelligence to perceive the truth to which Whitman and Kipling were blind: the 'voyage without' was useless unless the 'voyage within' had been successfully achieved. Otherwise the outward-bound traveller found nothing but an empty, unreal universe . . . at best 'a lighted empty hall'. A poem written shortly before his conversion to Catholicism announces Hopkins's deep conviction that only by a withdrawal from the outer world and a reconstruction of the inner life, can meaning and reality be given to sensuous experience:

> Shape nothing, lips; be lovely-dumb:
> It is the shut, the curfew sent
> From there where all surrenders come
> Which only makes you eloquent.

> Be shellèd, eyes, with double dark
> And find the uncreated light:
> This ruck and reel that you remark
> Coils, keeps, and teases simple sight.

Palate, the hutch of tasty lust,
Desire not to be rinsed with wine:
The can must be so sweet, the crust,
So fresh that come in fasts divine!

Nostrils, your careless breath that spend
Upon the stir and keep of pride,
What relish shall the censers send
Along the sanctuary side!

O feel-of-primrose hands, O feet
That want the yield of plushy sward,
But you shall walk the golden street
And you unhouse and house the Lord.

The adventure of the inner life for Hopkins was not merely a voyage but a reconstruction. He had to find there an 'uncreated light' which would give meaning and shape to the 'ruck and reel' of the material universe. It was here, certainly, that the rigorous ascetic discipline of the Jesuit training helped him. By his submission to that discipline he both gained and lost as a poet. He gained the enormous advantage of a disciplined inner life which was at the same time enriched by the traditional symbolism of a Church of age-old majesty and authority, enabling him to escape both the anarchic individualism of a Whitman and the unlovely Calvinism of a Kipling. On the other hand by becoming a Jesuit, he cut himself off from the main stream of contemporary English life and thought. A Jesuit in England has always been an exotic, and in the liberal-protestant England of the late nineteenth century, he was a kind of intellectual outcast without the glory of the martyrdom which would probably have been his fate three centuries before.

Hopkins had been a daring and original thinker on aesthetic problems while he was still at Oxford, and he was probably considerably affected by the teaching of Walter Pater, which he developed far more successfully than Oscar Wilde and the 'aesthetic' school. Already as an undergraduate at Oxford, he was using tentatively the terms 'inscape' and 'instress' which are the keys to his critical doctrine. The conception of 'inscape' is an aesthetic discovery of great importance. It arises from the realisation that for the artist a mere vague impression of natural beauty is unsatisfactory. 'Inscape' is the distinctive pattern perceived in nature by the artist, the 'species of individually-distinctive beauty'; it is what Clive Bell and later writers have called 'significant form'. 'Instress' is the effect on the artist's mind of the perception of 'inscape'. 'I saw the inscape freshly, as if my eye were still growing', he wrote in his Journal in 1872, 'though with a companion the eye and ear are for the most part shut and instress cannot come'. 'The perception of inscape', writes W. H. Gardner, 'is marked simultaneously as a rule with a flow of *instress*, as though the individual beholder becomes mystically one with the Whole'.

This aesthetic philosophy is a preparation for an art which will be based on a new synthesis of the outer and inner lives to replace that which had been achieved instinctively, in older cultures (as seen, for example, in that tradition of folk poetry which is the starting point of Hardy's poetry), and more consciously by the aristocratic 'bardic' tradition which was dead in England at the end of the nineteenth century. It is perhaps the only way in which the disintegration of the modern consciousness, which is the cause of the crisis in modern poetry can be overcome, but it is a way which is only open, in a modern industrialised society, to gifted individuals who are willing to submit themselves to an inner discipline as rigorous as that of the Jesuits. Hopkins perceived, moveover, that this new integration involved a revolution in poetic art. This was the revolution that the Pre-Raphaelites had glimpsed in the eighteen-fifties:

'Perfection is dangerous', he wrote in one of his notebooks, 'because it is deceptive. Art slips back while bearing in its distribution of tone, or harmony, the look of high civilisation, towards barbarism. Recovery must be a breaking up, a violence, such as was the Pre-Raphaelite School'. The last sentence might more accurately have ended, 'such as the Pre-Raphaelite School attempted but failed to carry out because of their lack of technical skill and speculative boldness'.

For the new poetry a new metre and a new diction were needed. The diction was not to be archaic like that of the nineteenth-century 'Parnassian' poetry descending from Milton and Dryden to Wordsworth and Tennyson:

'For it seems to me', he wrote to Bridges in 1879, 'that the poetical language of an age should be the current language heightened, to any degree heightened and unlike itself, but not (I mean normally: passing freaks and graces are another thing) an obsolete one'. The basis of the diction of poetry must be contemporary speech, but for the purposes of poetry this speech must be 'heightened' and even transformed out of all recognition.

The new metre was the now famous 'sprung rhythm' of which

the first suggestion is to be found in a letter written to Bridges as early as August 1868. It was a metre based on the counting of stresses instead of syllables in which feet could consist of a single stressed syllable or a stressed syllable with any number of unstressed or 'slack' syllables. Hopkins claimed that sprung rhythm had been used in Greek and Anglo-Saxon poetry and in traditional ballads and nursery rhymes. He used it, he said, 'because it is the nearest to the rhythm of prose, that is the native and natural rhythm of speech, the least forced, the most rhetorical and emphatic of all possible rhythms, combining, as it seems to me, markedness of rhythm—that is rhythm's self—and naturalness of expression'. It was, in fact, a metre which would have the flexibility of prose rhythm with a real pattern capable of endless subtleties and varieties. It would have all the freedom of Whitman's 'free verse' without its sprawling shapelessness.

   The first poem in which Hopkins put his new theories fully into practice was the *Deutschland* ode which is, perhaps, the first great religious poem in English since Milton.[1] It is also, in a sense, the first modern English poem. The opening stanzas are not only poetry of astonishing power; they are an invaluable revelation of the spiritual experience which produced that new integration of consciousness that was to be the basis of Hopkin's mature writing. They are an expression of the unmaking and remaking of his mind, ascribed to a God of transcendent power and majesty:

> Thou mastering me
>   God! giver of breath and bread;
> World's strand, sway of the sea
>   Lord of living and dead;
> Thou hast bound bones and veins in me, fastened me, flesh
> And after it almost unmade, what with dread,
>   Thy doing; and dost thou touch me afresh?
> Over again I feel thy finger and find thee.

In the fifth stanza the sensuous vision of the material world is transfigured by the 'instress' of a divine 'mystery' behind it:

> I kiss my hand
>   To the stars lovely asunder
> Starlight, wafting him out of it; and
>   Glow, glory in thunder;
> Kiss my hand to the dappled-with-damson west:

---

[1] 'Adonais' is a possible exception, if Shelley's pantheistic philosophy can be called a religion.

> Since, tho' he is under the world's splendour and wonder,
> His mystery must be instressed, stressed;
> For I greet him the days I meet him, and bless when I understand.

For the poet who wrote these lines an 'answering voice' has 'come from the skies'. Nature is no longer empty but filled with spiritual power.

The picture of the *Deutschland* sailing into the snowstorm in the thirteenth stanza is a striking example of Hopkins's new realism and his revolutionary use of language:

> Into the snows she sweeps,
> Hurling the haven behind,
> The Deutschland, on Sunday; and so the sky keeps,
> For the infinite air is unkind,
> And the sea flint-flake, black-backed in the regular blow,
> Sitting Eastnortheast, in cursed quarter, the wind;
> Wiry and white-fiery and whirlwind-swivellèd snow
> Spins to the widow-making unchilding unfathering deeps.

Alliteration, assonance and internal rhymes with new word-formations and unusual word-order all combine to make the reader not merely see the dim image of a ship in a storm, but feel the stress, the violence and the terror, and strange beauty of the storm. Hopkins is here anticipating James Joyce and Edith Sitwell in the attempt to create a new art of language which will rival music and painting in the immediacy of its sensuous effects and achieve that 'perfect identification of matter and form' of which Pater had prophesied in *The Renaissance.*[1]

The weakness of the *Wreck of the Deutschland* is a certain lack of the architectural unity required in a poem on a grand scale. The opening autobiographical section is among Hopkins's greatest achievements and the picture of the actual wreck is a triumph. There is grandeur too in the figure of the nun who called on the name of Christ and the magnificent image of the God who looked down on the martyrdom:

> thou Orion of light;
> Thy unchancelling poising palms were weighing the worth,
> Thou martyr-master: in thy sight
> Storm flakes were scroll-leaved flowers, lily showers—
> sweet heaven was astrew in them.

[1] See 'The School of Giorgione' in *The Renaissance* (library ed.), p. 139.

But the conceit which identifies the five nuns with Christ's wounds, 'cipher of suffering Christ' and the stigmata of 'Father Francis' has an exotic prettiness which recalls the baroque poetry and sculpture of the seventeenth century and is out of keeping with the dignity of the theme, while the assumption of the nun as a second Virgin at the end of the poem and the invocation asking for her intercession for the conversion of Britain seem a little over-strained and selfconscious. Nevertheless, all such weaknesses are obliterated by the overwhelming impression of power and majesty produced by the ode as a whole.

The writing of the *Deutschland* ode seems to have released a flood of creative power in Hopkins which produced his great nature poems of 1877. He had found a powerful stimulus in the doctrine of the medieval scholastic philosopher, Duns Scotus, whose works he seems to have first read when he was on a holiday in the Isle of Man in 1872. He was delighted with Scotus's 'principle of individuation' and his conception of 'haecceitas' or 'thisness' as the specific nature of a thing in virtue of which it differs from everything else and which he regards as the true bond between the creature and God. In this doctrine he found a means of reconciling his intense delight in the beauty and 'inscape' of material things and his equally intense religious experience. Thus he achieves a unity founded on a tension between opposites, and the apprehension of this unity filled him with joy of which the typical expression is to be found in 'Pied Beauty':

> Glory be to God for dappled things—
>   For skies of couple-colour as a brinded cow;
>   For rose-moles all in stipple upon trout that swim;
> Fresh-firecoal chestnut-falls; finches' wings;
>   Landscape plotted and pieced—fold, fallow and plough;
>   And áll trádes, their gear and tackle and trim.
>
> All things counter, original, spare, strange;
>   Whatever is fickle, freckled (who knows how?)
>   With swift, slow; sweet, sour; adazzle, dim;
> He fathers-forth whose beauty is past change:
>   Praise him.

Compare this poem with the lines from Whitman's 'Song of Myself' quoted above (see p. 54). Whitman's universalism is vague and sprawling like his metre; Hopkins's is concentrated and controlled by a philosophic principle. The poems written at this

time are full of ecstatic joy in the richness of nature and are brilliant
with glowing light and colour. They are written in a diction which
is neither the colourless standardised speech of urban, industrial
England nor the affected archaism of Victorian 'Parnassian' poetry.
It is contemporary colloquial English 'heightened' by the use of a
vocabulary that includes dialect and technical words and numerous
specially created compounds, a diction that is indeed sometimes
odd and grotesque but always full of vitality and power. Hopkins,
like the great Elizabethans, is using the whole resources of the
language and not merely a limited range of words and constructions
considered suitable for poetry.

The representative poem of this phase of Hopkins's development is the famous 'Windhover', the sonnet in which a kestrel
seen in flight on the downs becomes a symbol of all natural beauty,
which, by a sudden and dramatic transition, is compared with the
spiritual beauty of Christ's sacrifice. At the same time the bird's
flight seems to represent the poet's artistic sensibility contrasted
with and yet also linked to the austere self-sacrifice of the priestly
life which he had chosen:

> I caught this morning morning's minion, king-
> dom of daylight's dauphin, dapple-dawn-drawn Falcon, in his riding
> Of the rolling level underneath him steady air, and striding
> High there, how he rung upon the rein of a wimpling wing
> In his ecstasy! then off, off forth on swing
> As a skate's heel sweeps smooth on a bow-bend: the hurl and gliding
> Rebuffed the big wind. My heart in hiding
> Stirred for a bird,—the achieve of, the mastery of the thing!
>
> Brute beauty and valour and act, oh air, pride, plume, here
> Buckle! AND the fire that breaks from thee then, a billion
> Times told lovelier, more dangerous, O my chevalier!
>
> No wonder of it: shéer plód makes plough down sillion
> Shine, and blue-bleak embers, ah my dear,
> Fall, gall themselves, and gash gold-vermilion.

Hopkins called this sonnet 'the best thing I have ever done'. It
achieves that combination of realism with lyrical passion which
the Pre-Raphaelites sought both in their poetry and their painting.
Here is a writer who has picked up the threads which the young
William Morris had dropped nearly twenty years before and has
achieved poetry from which discursive argument and prose connections are eliminated. It is an art which sets poetic images before

C

the reader in their naked brilliance connected only by the logic of the imagination.

Hopkins was deeply moved by the ugliness and the injustice of the late Victorian England. In the great sonnet, 'God's Grandeur', he embodies his vision of the drabness and dullness of the industrial age in four lines which contain a searching criticism of a whole civilisation:

> Generations have trod, have trod, have trod;
>   And all is seared with trade; bleared, smeared with toil;
>   And wears man's smudge and shares man's smell: the soil
> Is bare now, nor can foot feel, being shod.

In a letter dated 2 August, 1871, he surprised and shocked Bridges by proclaiming that he was at heart a 'communist':

I am afraid some great revolution is not far off. Horrible to say, in a manner, I am a Communist. Their ideal bating some things is nobler than that professed by any secular statesman I know of . . . . Besides it is just. I do not mean the means of getting to it are. But it is a dreadful thing for the greatest and most necessary part of a very rich nation to live a hard life without dignity, knowledge, comforts, delight, or hopes in the midst of plenty—which plenty they make. They profess that they do not care what they wreck and burn, the old civilisation and order must be destroyed. This is a dreadful lookout but what has the old civilisation done for them? As it at present stands in England it is itself in great measure founded on wrecking. But they got none of the spoils, they came in for nothing but harm from it then and thereafter. England has grown hugely wealthy but this wealth has not reached the working classes; I expect it has made their condition worse. Besides this iniquitous order the old civilisation embodies another order mostly old and what is new in direct entail from the old, the old religion, learning, law, art, etc., and all the history that is preserved in standing monuments. But as the working classes have not been educated they know next to nothing of all this and cannot be expected to care if they destroy it. The more I look the more black and deservedly black the future looks. . . .

Hopkins's statement that 'Horrible to say, in a manner, I am a Communist' can be compared with the other statement that Walt Whitman's mind was 'more like my own than any man's living'. Stevenson's Dr Jekyll and Mr Hyde can be taken as a symbol of this poet. Dr Jekyll was the model Victorian scholar, the favourite pupil of Jowett, the friend of Newman and the saintly Catholic priest; Mr Hyde was the savage and sensual artist, akin to Walt

Whitman, that 'great scoundrel', and the 'communist' whose bitter and devastating criticism laid bare the hideous injustice on which the smooth life of cultivated English gentlefolk like Bridges was based. In some of Hopkins's most memorable poems the tension between these two sides of his mind is at once expressed and overcome. In the nature poems such as 'The Windhover' it is the tension between Hopkins the sensual artist and Hopkins the Christian. Hopkins the 'communist' with his burning sympathy for the toiling masses and Hopkins the priest with his ardent religious faith are reconciled in certain poems which arise from his contact with working men in the course of his parochial duties. The most memorable of these poems is the sonnet on 'Felix Randal':

> Felix Randal the farrier, O he is dead then? my duty all ended,
> Who have watched his mould of man, big-boned and hardy-handsome
> Pining, pining, till time when reason rambled in it and some
> Fatal four disorders, fleshed there all contended?
>
> Sickness broke him. Impatient he cursed at first, but mended
> Being anointed and all; though a heavenlier heart began some
> Months earlier, since I had our sweet reprieve and ransom
> Tendered to him. Ah well, God rest him all road ever he offended!
>
> This seeing the sick endears them to us, us too it endears.
> My tongue had taught thee comfort, touch had quenched thy tears
> Thy tears that touched my heart, child, Felix, poor Felix Randal;
>
> How far from then forethought of, all thy more boisterous years,
> When thou at the random grim forge, powerful amidst peers,
> Didst fettle for the great grey dray horse his bright and battering sandal!

Equally notable both as a technical experiment and as an expression of the poet's intense sympathy with common humanity is the pictorial poem 'Harry Ploughman' with its unforgettable impression of the ploughman at work:

> He leans to it, Harry bends, look. Back, elbow and liquid waist
> In him, all quail to the wallowing o' the plough:
>   's cheek crimsons; curls
> Wag or crossbridle, in a wind lifted, windlaced—
>   See his wind—lilylocks—laced;
> Churlsgrace, too, child of Amansstrength, how it hangs or hurls
> Them—broad in bluffhide his frowning feet lashed! raced
> With, along them, cragiron under and cold furls—
>   With-a-fountain's shining-shot furls.

The single poem in which Hopkins attempts direct social criticism
is the extremely packed and obscure 'caudated' sonnet 'Tom's
Garland: upon the Unemployed', which neither Bridges nor
Dixon could understand. Hopkins supplied an explanation which
is one of the most powerful passages in his prose writings. The
poem opens with a picture of two navvies Tom and Dick tramping
home to bed and supper. The poet then exclaims:

> Commonweal
> Little I reck ho! lacklevel in, if all had bread:
> What! Country is honour enough in all us—lordly head,
> With heaven's lights high hung round, or, mother-ground
> That mammocks, mighty foot. But no way sped
> Nor mind not mainstrength; gold go garlanded
> With, perilous, O no; nor yet plod safe shod sound;
> Undenizened, beyond bound
> Of earth's glory, earth's ease, all; no-one nowhere,
> In wide the world's weal; rare gold, bold steel, bare
> In both; care, but share care—
> This, by Despair, bred Hangdog dull; by Rage,
> Manwolf, worse; and their packs infest the age.

The explanation of this passage is an important piece of self-
revelation:

Here come a violent but effective hyperbaton or suspension, in which
the action of the mind mimics that of the labourer—surveys his lot, low
but free from care; then by a sudden strong act throws it over the shoulder
or tosses it away as a light matter. The witnessing of which lightheartedness
makes me indignant with the fools of Radical Levellers. But presently I
remember that this is all very well for those who are in, however low,
the Commonwealth and share in any way the common weal; but that
the curse of our times is that many do not share it, that they are outcasts
from it and have neither security nor splendour; that they share care with
high and obscurity with the low, but wealth or comfort with neither.
And this state of things, I say, is the origin of Loafers, Tramps, Corner-boys,
Roughs, Socialists and other pests of society.

Here Dr Jekyll dismisses the 'Radical Levellers' with indignation but
Mr Hyde finds that there is much in the arguments of these 'pests
of society'. Hopkins clearly perceived that the England of his day
was suffering from a serious social malady. His natural sympathy
for revolutionary views is partly repressed by the intense conservatism of his class and his church and the result is an unresolved

conflict to which the obscurity of the sonnet may be partly due. At the end of one of his most suggestive and tantalising fragments we hear the voice of the half-suppressed revolutionary poet:

> O but I bear my burning witness though
> Against the wild and wanton work of men.

In 'Tom's Garland, Harry Ploughman', and the beautiful unfinished 'Epithalamium' written in Ireland in the eighteen-eighties, Hopkins's experiments in language and metre were pushed to their furthest limits. He believed that 'declaimed the strange constructions would be dramatic and effective'. But there was no one to declaim them and no one to listen if they had been declaimed. He was discouraged by the fact that 'Tom's Garland' was incomprehensible even to poets like Bridges and Dixon, and he wrote, 'I must go no further on this road'. A revolution in poetry such as Hopkins planned cannot be carried out by a single writer in isolation. 'What I want', he wrote in one of his last letters, '. . . to be more intelligible, smoother and less singular, is an audience'.

He had plans for poems on a grand scale. In 1881 he was meditating a 'great ode' on Edmund Campion, the Elizabethan Jesuit and he also planned tragedies on St Winifred, the Welsh Saint, and Margaret Clitheroe, an Elizabethan Catholic who was martyred in 1586. He wrote a few scattered stanzas of the ode, 'something between the *Deutschland* and "Alexander's Feast",' which unfortunately have not survived. It had to be abandoned because the 'vein soon dried' as a result of the 'slavery of mind or heart' imposed on him by his work in Liverpool and Glasgow. Of 'Margaret Clitheroe' only two lyrical fragments survive but of the tragedy of 'St Winifred's Well' there are three noble passages in alexandrine blank verse and a great ode to be sung by a chorus of maidens, 'The Leaden Echo and the Golden Echo'. This choric ode and the enlarged 'sonnet'— 'That Nature is a Heraclitean Fire and of the comfort of the Resurrection' are Hopkins's two most ambitious attempts to treat themes of cosmic vastness. 'The Leaden Echo and the Golden Echo' is, perhaps, his greatest technical achievement. He wrote of this poem to Dixon, 'I have never done anything more musical'. He came nearer in this poem than in any of his works to using language as pure incantation. The music here is gentle and flowing and there are none of the abrupt transitions or violent contrasts so common in this poetry. In the first half of the poem, the 'Leaden Echo', all the beauties of the senses are seen fading into old age, corruption and death:

> wisdom is early to despair:
> Be beginning; since, no, nothing can be done
> To keep at bay
> Age and age's evils, hoar hair,
> Ruck and wrinkle, drooping, dying, deaths' worst, winding
>   sheets, tombs, worms and tumbling to decay.

It ends with a fourfold repetition of the word 'despair', the last syllable of which is echoed by the second semi-chorus ('The Golden Echo') as 'spare' and from this point all the beauty which had faded in the 'Leaden Echo' comes back with a great rush of sound, and is shown as preserved by the one 'catch or key' which can ward off death and decay, the way which is:

>   not within seeing of the sun,
>   Not within the singeing of the strong sun,
>   Tall sun's tingeing, or treacherous the tainting of the earth's air.

It is the way of surrender to God, 'beauty's self and beauty's giver', who keeps all that is freely forfeited with a fonder care than we could have kept it. The ode ends with a renewed questioning. If beauty is really so kept for us, why are men 'so haggard at the heart, so care-coiled, care-killed, so fagged, so fashed, so cogged, so cumbered'? At the end of the poem question and answer seem to fade away into dim attitudes beyond human reach:

>   Where kept? Do but tell us where kept, where.—
>   Yonder.—what high as that! We follow, now we follow—
>   Yonder yes, yonder, yonder,
>   Yonder.

The same themes of mortality and deliverance are treated in a very different way in the 'sonnet' on the 'Heraclitean Fire'. Here the starting point is the famous 'flux' of Heraclitus, the early Greek philosopher (who said 'all things are flowing'), translated into terms of a stormy skyscape and landscape painted with the savage energy of a Van Gogh. Nowhere has Hopkins used language with such splendid richness and power as in this poem. The clouds are 'heaven-roysterers, in gay-gangs', 'delightfully the bright wind boisterous ropes, wrestles'. But all this splendour is only 'nature's bonfire' burning away to nothingness and even man, regarded as part of nature, 'manshape, that shone sheer off, disseveral, a star', is blotted out by death. The poem ends with one of the finest of

all Hopkins's abrupt dramatic transitions. The resurrection, coming
with a sudden blare of music and blaze of light, transforms death
into glory, and man into the 'immortal diamond' of Christ:

>   Flesh fade, and mortal trash
> Fall to the residuary worm; world's wildfire, leave but ash:
>   In a flash, at a trumpet crash,
> I am all at once what Christ is, since he was what I am, and
> This Jack, joke, poor potsherd, patch, matchwood, immortal diamond,
>   Is immortal diamond.

The integration or 'unity of life' achieved by Hopkins in all the
poems hitherto noticed is a unity which includes the artist who is
concerned with sensuous beauty and the ardent believer in catholic
Christianity. All these poems (except the purely pictorial 'Harry
Ploughman' and the exceptional 'Tom's Garland') imply the
presence of a God of infinite goodness and beauty in nature and
the deliverance of man from death by faith in Christ. All, indeed,
are full of excited joy at the meaning and reality given to nature
by these religious concepts. But in the last years of his life Hopkins
wrote poetry of a very different kind. It is to be found in the
poems that Bridges called 'the terrible posthumous sonnets'. In
these works the tension by which 'unity of life' was maintained in
the earlier works seems to have snapped. The creative artist was
starved by the want of an audience and suffered agony from his
isolation and enslavement to uncongenial work. His poetry is full
no longer of hope and joy but of misery and despair. He is still,
indeed, a sincere believer but he no longer exults in the presence
of God in nature or in man's deliverance from mortality by divine
aid. In these poems God is shown as indifferent to the poet's
sufferings, almost as an enemy:

> But ah, but O thou terrible, why wouldst thou rude on me
> Thy wring-world right foot rock? Lay a lionlimb against me? scan
> With darksome devouring eyes by bruised bones? and fan,
> O in turns of tempest, me heaped there; me frantic to avoid thee and flee?

Now the Jesuit Hopkins expresses 'the schism in the soul' of modern
man with an intensity equal to that of the agnostic Hardy and far
excelling that of the atheist Housman:

> No worst, there is none. Pitched past pitch of grief,
> More pangs will, schooled at forepangs, wilder wring.

Comforter, where, where is your comforting?
Mary, mother of us, where is your relief?
My cries heave, herds-long; huddle in a main, a chief
Woe, world-sorrow; in an age-old anvil wince and sing—
Then lull, then leave off. Fury had shrieked 'No ling-
ering! Let me be fell: force I must be brief.'

O the mind, mind has mountains; cliffs of fall
Frightful, sheer, no-man-fathomed. Hold them cheap
May who ne'er hung there. Nor does long our small
Durance deal with that steep or deep. Here! creep,
Wretch, under a comfort serves in a whirlwind: all
Life death does end and each day dies with sleep.

In these last tragic poems of Hopkins, his endless experiments,
his love of elaborate technique and artifice disappear, and are
replaced by a new starkness and clarity, 'the terrible crystal' as
Dixon called it, of his later style. They are among the great tragic
utterances of the modern crisis, representing not only the agony
of the dying priest to whom his religion brought no comfort, but
the complaint of modern humanity finding itself isolated in a
hostile or indifferent universe and faced with the horror of spiritual
disharmony. The last of the 'terrible sonnets' ends with a bitter
contrast between the fruitfulness of nature and the sterility of man
in the modern world. Here Hopkins anticipates the image of
drought used for the same purpose by T. S. Eliot over thirty years
later:

See, banks and brakes
Now, leavèd how thick! lacèd they are again
With fretty chervil, look, and fresh wind shakes
Them; birds build—but not I build; no, but strain,
Time's eunuch, and not breed one work that wakes.
Mine, O thou lord of life, send my roots rain.

Hopkins tried to carry out, single handed, a revolution in poetic
art which would have taxed the energies of a dozen geniuses.
More clearly than any man of his time, he understood the real
nature of the crisis in English poetry and the means by which it
could be overcome. They were first a religion or philosophy which
would be a true modern myth and give the poet a new 'unity of
life', an integration of spiritual and sensuous experience, and
secondly, the adoption of sweeping reforms in technique which
would give fresh vitality to the language and metre of English

poetry. He achieved 'unity of life' but at a great cost. The price that he paid was submission to a rigorous religious discipline which involved isolation from his fellow countrymen, enslavement to uncongenial work and finally the tragic collapse expressed in his last poems, and his premature death. Moreover the literary public of his day, under the guidance of elegant practitioners of belles-lettres like Lang and Gosse (the 'trioleteers' as he called them) was quite unprepared to accept his revolutionary technical innovations, which were, in fact, remedies for maladies the very existence of which they did not recognize. So Hopkins lived and died in obscurity, and his poetry, as he himself recognised, suffered by his isolation.

Nevertheless his heroic enterprise was not wasted. Since the publication of his poems in 1918 they have provided an invaluable example and inspiration to the poets of the twentieth century and their influence is by no means exhausted. In many respects the late Victorian Jesuit is still in advance of his numerous imitators who lack the scholarship, the disciplined inner life and the profound understanding of the principles of aesthetics which lie behind his revolutionary experiments.

Hopkins's friend Robert Bridges (1844–1930) was a fine poet whose work was at one time overestimated by academic critics and then unfairly disparaged by enthusiastic admirers of Hopkins in the nineteen-twenties and 'thirties. Bridges is not a poet of the modern crisis except with regard to his metrical innovations. He was rather the last authentic example of the aristocratic Victorian artist in verse, whose work sprang from the life of a leisured and highly cultivated class of gentlefolk. At Eton he had already decided that what interested him was 'the inexhaustible satisfaction of form, the magic of speech, lying as it seemed to me in the masterly control of material'. 'It was', he adds, 'an art which I hoped to learn'. Like Hopkins he came to Oxford a high churchman or Puseyite, intending to take holy orders. However, he soon abandoned both his ritualism and his intention to become a priest. After leaving Oxford he travelled in Italy and the East, and then studied medicine and worked as a hospital physician until 1881, when, after a serious illness, he retired to Yattendon and devoted himself wholly to literature. His first volume of poems appeared in 1873 and his collected *Shorter Poems* in 1890. His reputation as a poet grew steadily in the early twentieth century. He was appointed Poet Laureate by the Asquith government on the death of Alfred Austin in 1910, and his house at Boar's Hill near Oxford became

a place of pilgrimage for young writers in the years immediately
following the First World War.

Bridges's early lyrics are remarkable for their fastidious delicacy
of form and their freedom from the influence of the great Victorean
poets. He was a lover of old English music and many of his early
lyrics are obviously influenced by the Elizabethan madrigalists,
especially Thomas Campion, and also by the young Milton, and
the Blake of *Poetical Sketches*. In his most characteristic poems he
is not an explorer either of the inner or the outer life but an exquisite
craftsman in verse with a peculiar gift for verbal melody. 'He gave',
wrote Yeats, 'to lyric poetry a new cadence, a distinction as deliberate as that of Whistler's painting, an impulse moulded and checked
like that in certain poems of Landor, but different, more in the
nerves, less in the blood, more birdlike, less human':

> I heard a linnet courting
> His lady in the spring:
> His mates were idly sporting,
> Nor stayed to hear him sing
>   His song of love.—
> I fear my speech distorting
>   His tender love.

Yeats's comment on this stanza is acute: 'Every metaphor, every
thought a commonplace, emptiness everywhere, the whole
magnificent'. As far as Bridges was concerned, industrial England
might never have existed. At the time of the General Strike of
1926 he said to Edward Thompson, 'The old ship's going down!
And I'm going down with it!' Thompson quotes Professor G. N.
Clark's comment on this remark: 'He's thinking of the fellows on
the quarter-deck! Not the poor devils down in the engine-room!'
Bridges's poems are decidedly poetry of the 'quarter-deck' and a
very pleasant place it is, a world of gentle English landscapes, clear
streams, downlands, gardens and birdsong, haunted by memories
of the classics, of music and poetry and decorous Victorian love-
making. But as Yeats remarked, there is an emptiness in it, which
is particularly noticeable whenever Bridges tries to deal with a
simple human theme as in the very flat, sentimental poem called
'The Villager', which can be contrasted with Hopkins's 'Felix
Randal' (see above, p. 65).

> There was no lad handsomer than Willie was
> The day that he came to father's house.

> There was non had an eye as soft an' blue
> As Willie's was, when he came to woo.

> To a labouring life though bound thee be,
> An' I on my father's ground live free,
> I'll take thee, I said, for thy manly grace,
> Thy gentle voice an' thy loving face.

The threadbare diction and lifeless rhythm of this poem reflect the mind of an upper class which has lost touch with common humanity and can only see it as a sentimental abstraction.

The most interesting of *The Shorter Poems*, however, are those affected by the experiments of Hopkins to whose memory Bridges dedicated his second book of shorter poems. In these poems, such as the much-anthologised 'A Passer by', the beautiful 'London Snow,' 'The Downs', and others, Bridges makes cautious attempts to loosen the traditional syllabic metre of English library verse and to write, in his own words, 'by the rules of a new prosody', a novelty which, he states in a note prefixed to the edition of 1880, 'is almost entirely due to a friend, whose poems remain in manuscript'. The best of Bridges's tentative experiments in sprung rhythm are poems of landscape, which he paints with the delicacy and distinction of a Whistler or a Sisley, but without the dynamism or monumental quality of a Hopkins·or a Cézanne.

> O bold majestic downs, smooth, fair and lonely;
> O still solitude, only matched in the skies:
>   Perilous in steep places,
>   Soft in the level races,
> Where sweeping in phantom silence the cloudland flies;
> With lovely undulation of fall and rise;
>   Entrenched with thickets thorned,
> By delicate miniature dainty flowers adorned.

These experiments in the 'new prosody' in Bridges's *Shorter Poems* had an important effect on writers of the earlier twentieth century like Walter de la Mare and others. They began the process of loosening the traditional rhythms of English verse which was greatly accelerated by the publication of Hopkins's poems in 1918.

Bridges was a remarkable prosodist (the first, perhaps, in England who had a grasp of phonetic theory) and a tireless experimenter in verse forms. He wrote in 1912 'that anyone can see that serious rime is now exhausted in English verse or that Milton's blank verse practically ended as a serious form with Milton.'[1] He experimented for some time with classical quantitative metres, following the theories of his friend W. J. Stone. In the last phase of his work he used a flexible twelve syllable line with great variation in the placing of the accents, which he claimed to be the descendant of Milton's 'counter-pointed' verse in 'Samson Agonistes'. With this metre he adopted a more colloquial and less 'Parnassian' diction that in his early poems. Here again he is most successful as a writer of pure lyric as in the flowerlike daintiness of 'Cheddar Pinks' or the crystal-line serenity of 'Christmas 1913':

> A frosty Christmas Eve
>   when the stars were shining
> Fared I forth alone
>   where westward falls the hill,
> And from many a village
>   in the water'd valley
> Distant music reach'd me
>   peals of bells aringing:
> The constellated sounds
>   ran sprinkling on earth's floor
> As the dark vault above
>   with stars was spangled o'er.

His long work, *The Testament of Beauty* is an ambitious attempt at a philosophic poem on a grand scale in the 'loose alexandrines', as he called his new metre. In contains passages and single lines of great nobility and beauty, but the Platonic myth of the 'chariot of the soul' is not imagined with sufficient distinctness and power to provide an adequate framework and the attempted fusion of idealistic philosophy with modern scientific thought is neither wholly convincing in itself nor always sufficiently transmuted into poetic material.

As a lyric and a philosophic poet Bridges is the last of the Great Victorians. His contribution to a new English poetry is confined to his original and suggestive work as an experimenter in metrical forms.

---

[1] 'Wordsworth and Kipling' in *Collected Essays*, Vol II, p. 30.

4

YEATS AND SYNGE

In 1886, when Hopkins was Professor of Greek in the University College of Dublin, an Irish painter showed him some poems by his son, then a young man of twenty-one. The painter was John Butler Yeats, a member of an old Irish Protestant family, a friend and admirer of the English Pre-Raphaelites, and a man of singular wisdom and tolerance. The son was the poet William Butler Yeats (1865–1939). The elder Yeats had encouraged his son to read Blake, Shelley, Keats, Morris and Rossetti. The boy spent his holidays with his mother's relatives, the Pollexfens and Middletons in County Sligo in the West of Ireland, and there from early childhood he had been in touch with a truly popular culture. It was a world where personality still counted for much and where men were valued rather for what they were than for their possessions. His grandfather Pollexfen was an impressive person whom the poet thought he 'confused with God' in his childhood. 'Even today', he wrote in *Reveries* (1914), 'when I read *King Lear* his image is always before me and I often wonder if the delight in passionate men in my plays and in my poetry is more than his memory'. Yeats's mother 'read no books, but she and the fisherman's wife would tell each other stories that Homer might have told, pleased with any moment of sudden intensity and laughing together over any point of satire'. Mary Battle, his uncle's servant, 'could neither read nor write and her mind, which answered his gloom with its merriment, was rammed with every sort of old history and strange belief'. Near his uncle's home in Sligo was the island of Innisfree in Lough Gill, said to be an enchanted place, where the boy planned to live one day alone in a cottage.

After leaving school the young Yeats attended an art school in Dublin, but he made little progress in painting. He wrote much poetry influenced by Spenser and Shelley, including a verse drama, *Mosada*, which his father had privately printed. At the time, too, he began those explorations of the occult which lasted throughout his life. He was initiated into Indian theosophy by a Brahmin, Mohini Chaterjee, whose teaching inspired several of his early poems. He also made the acquaintance of the old Irish revolutionary, John O'Leary, by whom he was profoundly influenced. Under O'Leary's guidance he became an Irish nationalist, but his nationalism was literary and artistic rather than political. It was the nationalism of which he wrote later in 'To Ireland in the Coming Times':

> Know, that I would accounted be
> True brother of that company,
> Who sang to sweeten Ireland's wrong,
> Ballad and story, rann and song;
> Nor be I any less than of them,
> Because the red-rose-bordered hem
> Of her, whose history began
> Before God made the angelic clan,
> Trails all about the written page. . . .

When he was still a young man he began to conceive a plan for bringing together the two halves of Ireland so as to build a 'unity of life' that would produce a great literature: 'I began to plot and scheme how one might seal with the right image the soft wax before it began to harden. I had noticed that the Irish Catholics, among whom had been born so many political martyrs, had not the good taste, the household courtesy and decency of Protestant Ireland I had known, and yet Protestant Ireland had begun to think of nothing but getting on. I thought we might bring the halves together if we had a national literature that made Ireland beautiful in the memory, and yet had been freed from provincialism by an exacting criticism, and European pose.' It was an ambitious and noble plan, but the young Yeats did not realise then, as he wrote much later on, that 'the modern world is more powerful than any propaganda, that no nation can isolate itself from the crisis of the modern world', and that even a small nation with a living folk culture was too deeply penetrated by the vulgarity of commercialism and the spiritual emptiness of the industrial age to recover the integrated life of which he dreamed.

The Yeatses moved to London in 1887. There the young poet compiled Irish folk tales for London publishers, contributed poems to English periodicals, including Henley's *Scots Observer* (afterward *The National Observer*) and in collaboration with Edward Ellis edited Blake's *Prophetic Books*. In 1888, with financial help from O'Leary, he published his first book of verse containing a narrative poem, *The Wanderings of Oisin* and a number of shorter pieces. Three years later he was attending the meetings of the Rhymers' Club at the Cheshire Cheese with Lionel Johnson, Ernest Dowson, Arthur Symons, and the other writers of the Tragic Generation. These are men whom he called

> Poets with whom I learned my trade,
> Companions of the Cheshire Cheese.

He admired Dowson's lyrics, but was most influenced by Lionel Johnson and Arthur Symons. Johnson introduced him to the writings of Pater and gave him new ideals of scholarship and intellectual distinction. Symons's wide knowledge of contemporary French literature was of great value to him and it was through Symons that he came to know the work of Mallarmé and the doctrines of symbolism.

Two women played an important part in the development of Yeats's genius. One was Maud Gonne, the orphan daughter of an Anglo-Irish colonel, who had become a fierce political agitator. She failed to convert Yeats to her extremist views, but her beauty and her passionate idealism fascinated him throughout his life and were the inspiration of much of his poetry. The other was Lady Augusta Gregory, the middle-aged widow of a great landowner in the West of Ireland, a woman of considerable literary ability with a great enthusiasm for the arts and a wide knowledge of Irish legend and folklore. Yeats stayed with her often at her beautiful house at Coole in County Galway. Through her generosity he was able to escape the drudgery of earning his living by journalism; she also took him to visit the cottages of the Galway peasants and thus enabled him to renew that fruitful contact with folk culture which he had known in his youth in Sligo. With Lady Gregory, Edward Martyn and George Moore, the novelist, at the beginning of the new century he started the famous literary theatre in Dublin which was to be the focal point of a great Irish literary renaissance. They were soon joined by John Millington Synge (1871–1909), a

young Irishman whom Yeats had found living in a garret in Paris
and had advised to seek fresh inspiration by going to live among
the peasants in the Aran Islands in the far west of Ireland.

Yeats's early poetry was strongly influenced by Morris and the
Pre-Raphaelites but it had an other-worldliness which comes
from Celtic legend and a peculiar kind of simplicity derived from
the folk culture of the Irish peasants. The poems that made him
famous were the lyrics first published by Henley in *The Scots
Observer* and reprinted with *The Wanderings of Oisin* (1888) and
the collection called *The Rose* printed with *The Countess Cathleen*
in 1893. They are dreamy romantic lyrics, 'To an Island in the
Water', 'The Madness of King Goll', 'The Lake Island of Innisfree',
'The Sorrow of Love', 'When you are old' and others, some of
which were afterwards suppressed. These poems found a ready
response in England, perhaps as an antidote to the blatant and
brassy vulgarity of Kipling. The writer of them is a belated Pre-
Raphaelite, as Dr Bowra writes, 'a good pupil of William Morris,
a poet of escape, singer of music in the deep heart's core'. R. L.
Stevenson wrote from Samoa to congratulate the young poet. He
said of 'Innisfree' 'It is so quaint and airy, simple, artful, and
eloquent to the heart'. In 1895 Fisher Unwin published a one volume
edition of Yeats's poems containing *The Wanderings of Usheen*,
The Countess Cathleen, *The Land of Heart's Desire* and a number of
lyrics including *Innisfree*. It had a prettily decorated binding and
a design in the manner of Walter Crane on the title page. It was
reprinted several times and its author might easily have become a
sort of Irish Stevenson, a pet of the section of the English middle class
which wanted to forget the ugliness and vulgarity of industrial civilisation and escape into the mists of an imaginary Celtic Twilight.[1]

It was largely the influence of the men of the Tragic Generation
that prevented Yeats from becoming a facile popular poet. He was
less influenced by their poetry than by their whole-hearted devotion
to their art. He acknowledged the debt handsomely later on in
the poem called 'The Grey Rock':

> You had to face your ends when young—
> 'Twas wine or women, or some curse—
> But never made a poorer song
> That you might have a heavier purse,
> Nor gave loud service to a cause

[1] This term was first used by Yeats as the title of a collection of Irish peasan.
tales (1893).

> That you might have a troop of friends.
> You kept the Muses' sterner laws,
> And unreprenting faced your ends,
> And therefore earned the right—and yet
> Dowson and Johnson most I praise—
> To troop with those the world's forgot,
> And copy their proud steady gaze.

However, the young Yeats had a great advantage over men like Johnson, Dowson and Symons. Unlike them, he was in touch with a genuine living folk culture and a mythology which had not grown stale and hackneyed by centuries of repetition. None of the other Rhymers could have written a poem like 'Down by the Salley Gardens', which was produced like many of Burns's lyrics by building on a few lines of folk-song.[1]

> Down by the salley gardens my love and I did meet;
> She passed the salley gardens with little snow-white feet.
> She bid me take love easy, as the leaves grow on the tree;
> But I, being young and foolish, with her would not agree.
>
> In a field by the river my love and I did stand,
> And on my leaning shoulder she laid her snow-white hand,
> She bid me take life easy, as the grass grows on the weirs,
> But I was young and foolish, and now am full of tears.

The mythology which Yeats used extensively in his early poems was the great body of Gaelic heroic legend which had been presented to English readers of the late eighteenth century in the faked prose 'epics' of Ossian by the Scottish schoolmaster Macpherson, and which was available for a young poet a hundred years later in the more scholarly and authentic versions published by Standish O'Grady and Douglas Hyde. This mythology had never been wholly forgotten in Ireland and for the young Yeats it had the fascination that Greek mythology had for the men of the Renaissance. For him it was no mere antiquarianism but something which he wholly absorbed and made part of his imaginative life as Milton absorbed the Hebrew sagas and Keats the Greek myths. 'Might I not', he wrote, 'with health and good luck to aid me, create some new *Prometheus Unbound*, Patrick or Columbkell, Oisin or Finn in Prometheus' stead, and instead of Caucasus, Cro-Patrick or Ben

---

[1] Yeats wrote of this poem that it was 'an extension of three lines sung to me by an old woman at Bally Sodare'.

Bulben?' This ambition to treat heroic themes on a large scale was very different from the spirit of the English Rhymers with their concentration on short, highly wrought poems. In 1905, he complained that 'modern literature and above all poetical literature is monotonous in its structure and effeminate in its continual insistence on certain moments of strained lyricism.' His own much-anthologised early lyrics include exquisite examples of this strained lyricism. When, for instance, in 'When you are old' he pictures Maud Gonne as an old woman nodding by the fire, he hears her

> bending down beside the glowing bars,
> Murmur, a little sadly, how love fled
> And paced upon the mountains overhead
> And hid his face amid a crowd of stars.

This rather precious and irrelevant image is really less effective than the classic commonplace of the sonnet of Ronsard which he is imitating:

> Vous serez au fouyer une vieille accroupie,
> Regrettant mon amour et vostre fier desdain.
> Vivez, si m'en croyez, n'attendez à demain:
> Cueillez dès aujourd'hui, les roses de la vie.[1]

As John Davidson recognized, there was, however, in the young Irishman too much 'blood and guts' for him to remain satisfied for long with poetry of this kind.

Very early in his career he attempted to treat legendary material on a large scale. *The Wanderings of Oisin* is a long romantic narrative poem full of echoes of Morris, Shelley, Coleridge, Keats and Sir Samuel Fergusson. As he admitted later, 'it has the overcharged colour inherited from the romantic movement'. Yet the mythology of Niam and Angus, the Fenians and the Danaans is fresh and has 'the beauty and wonder of altogether new things'. Moreover, the conflict between the old Celtic bard, Oisin (Macpherson's 'Ossian') and St Patrick is no mere piece of romantic antiquarianism but a symbol of a permanent and unresolved conflict in the European mind between the ideal of the artist and that of religion.

---

[1] Crouching beside your fire, a poor old crone, one day,
You will recall my love and your disdain with sorrow:
Ah, be advised, and live your life; heed not the morrow.
Henceforth resolve to pluck life's roses while you may.

The same theme is treated dramatically in the short play called *The Land of Heart's Desire* where the conflict is placed in a peasant setting. The struggle for the soul of the girl Mary Bruin is a tragic theme because it is a struggle between two powers both of which are respected by the poet:

> The Child: But I can lead you, newly married bride,
>   Where nobody gets old and crafty and wise,
>   Where nobody gets old and godly and grave,
>   Where nobody gets old and bitter of tongue,
>   And where kind tongues bring no captivity;
>   For we are but obedient to the thoughts
>   That drift into the mind at a wink of the eye.
> Father Hart: By the dear Name of the One Crucified,
>   I bid you, Mary Bruin, come to me.
> The Child: I keep you in the name of your own heart.

Yeats always preferred the world of the poetic imagination to the world of religion, but he knew that Mary Bruin's choice was a dangerous one. From the beginning his faery world was not the tinsel of the English Victorian imagination, but a world which was at once terrible and beautiful. The delicate clear music of the famous faery song in this play is the work of a great lyric poet:

> The wind blows out of the gates of the day,
> The wind blows over the lonely of heart,
> And the lonely of heart is withered away.

The Countess Cathleen, his first full length play, was originally written when he was little more than a boy but was repeatedly altered and revised. It is in the traditional English Shakespearian form and is full of Pre-Raphaelite decoration. Nevertheless, there are also touches of sharp realism which contrast with the literary flavour of the speeches about Celtic mythology:

> God and the Mother of God have dropped asleep.
> What do they care, he says, though the whole land
> Squeal like a rabbit under a weasel's tooth.
>   . . . .
> What can we do but live on sorrel and dock,
> And dandelion, till our mouths are green.

The Countess is a highly idealised Maud Gonne and Aleel the

Poet is doubtless an equally idealised Yeats, but the central theme
is no mere romantic fancy. The demon merchants who buy the
souls of the starving peasants clearly represent the commercialism
of Yeats's own day which was corrupting the minds of men all
over Europe, and Shemus's mad song, when he has sold his soul,
is the work of a poet who had already grasped the significance of
the crisis of the modern world.

> There's money for a soul, sweet yellow money.
> There's money for men's souls, good money, money.

Yeats began as a late romantic and Pre-Raphaelite with the
additional advantage of contact with Irish mythological tradition
and folk culture. What is remarkable about his whole career is his
sustained power of development. He could not remain a poet of
the Celtic Twilight. In the second phase of his work represented
by *The Wind among the Reeds* (1899) and *The Shadowy Waters*
(1900) he is making the 'voyage within', withdrawing as much as
possible from the contemporary world and enriching his inner life
by concentrating on purely visionary themes. This phase of his
work is comparable with Hopkins's arduous spiritual training as a
Jesuit. The religion which served as a means to purify and intensify
Yeats's inner life was symbolism and the high priest of the great
French symbolist movement was Stephane Mallarmé. Yeats was
never a good French scholar but Arthur Symons's translations of
Mallarmé's poems were as useful to him as Golding's Ovid was to
Shakespeare. Mallarmé's religion was an austere worship of
absolute beauty, which was to be reached by the rapt contemplation
of symbols. His poetry is a poetry of suggestion from which all
prosaic elements are banished. As Dr Bowra has written, 'All
preliminaries, explanations, comparisons are omitted and the gain
in concentration is enormous. The poetry is fully packed. It has
some of the direct appeal of music'. Unfortunately Mallarmé had
to create his own symbols, as the traditional symbols of religion
and mythology were dulled and hackneyed in the France of his
time. So when he shows us such an image as

> De l'éternel azur la sereine ironie

we can enjoy the music of the words and a sort of impalpable
music of ideas—the connection between serenity, irony and the
colour blue, but it is obvious that 'azur' means something for the
poet which can be understood only by the initiated. It is not a

great universal myth but a private mythology to which the 'common reader' has no clue.

Yeats accepted wholeheartedly Mallarmé's conception of 'pure' poetry. In his essay on 'The Symbolism of Poetry' he called for 'a return to the way of our fathers, a casting out of descriptions of nature for the sake of nature, of the moral law for the sake of the moral law, a casting out of all anecdotes and of that brooking over scientific opinion that so often extinguished the central flame in Tennyson'.

He wanted to 'cast out of serious poetry those energetic rhythms, as of a man running, which are the invention of the will with its eyes always on something to be done or undone' and to 'seek out those wavering, meditative organic rhythms, which are the embodiment of the imagination, that neither desires nor hates, because it had done with time'. His poetry was to be composed of 'words . . . as subtle, as complex, as full of mysterious life, as the body of a flower or of a woman'.

Instead of the private symbols of Mallarmé, which are always, in part, at least, unintelligible, Yeats uses the images of Celtic mythology in his symbolic poems. These are at once more precise than Mallarmé's inventions and also have a richness of association which Mallarmé's symbols lacked. In his earlier works Yeats had used the ancient Irish myths simply as stories; in the poems in *The Wind Among the Reeds* he uses them to express his own states of mind. Thus in 'The Song of Wandering Aengus' he takes the story of the ancient Irish hero who dreamed of a wonderfully beautiful maiden and searched for her throughout Ireland.[1] Yeats turns the story into a symbol (not an allegory) of the search of the poet for an unattainable beauty:

> Though I am old with wandering
> Through hollow lands and hilly lands,
> I will find out where she is gone,
> And kiss her lips and take her hands;
> And walk among long dappled grass,
> And pluck till time and times are done
> The silver apples of the moon.
> The golden apples of the sun.

This poem contains echoes of Morris's 'Nymph's Song to Hylas',

[1] See Dorothy Hoare, *The Works of Morris and Yeats in Relation to Saga Literature*, pp. 166-171.

but it is at once more precise and richer in texture than Morris's vague, nostalgic poem. The symbolism is perfectly intelligible but it has the magic of songs and is not dimmed by any prosaic moralising. In some poems, however, in this collection Yeats uses symbols which have no precise or intelligible meaning but which live by their own power and intensity. Such a poem is 'The Cap and the Bells' which is founded on a dream. No intellectual meaning can be attached to this jester who sends his soul in the shape of 'a straight blue garment' and his heart in the shape of 'a red and quivering garment' to the young queen. Nevertheless it is an impressive and moving poem and the symbols have a great emotional intensity:

> 'I have cap and bells', he pondered,
> 'I will send them to her and die';
> And when the morning whitened
> He left them where she went by.

> She laid them upon her bosom,
> Under a cloud of her hair,
> And her red lips sang them a love-song:
> Till stars grew out of the air.

In his note on 'The Cap and the Bells', Yeats wrote, 'The poem has always meant a great deal to me, though, as it is the way with symbolic poems, it has not always meant quite the same thing. Blake would have said, "the authors are in eternity", and I am quite sure they can only be questioned in dreams.' This note shows that Yeats's symbolism (unlike that of Mallarmé) is connected with a belief in occult influences and magic.

Yeats's most ambitious and elaborate symbolist work is the dramatic poem called *The Shadowy Waters*. He tried to adapt it for performance on the stage but never succeeded. It is essentially undramatic, a magnificent lyric in dialogue where all the characters speak with the voice of the poet. The image of a pirate ship sailing into unknown seas had haunted Yeats from his boyhood. The story of the pirate Forgael, the queen Dectora whom he captures and bewitches and the birds with human heads who follow his ship has no meaning that can be translated into intellectual terms, but like the jester and the queen in 'The Cap and the Bells' these characters are highly successful symbols of emotional states that defy analysis. *The Shadowy Waters* is a great hymn to the romantic

conception of a love that passes human understanding. It is the love
of which Forgael speaks to Aibric:

> Now the secret's out;
> For it is love that I am seeking for,
> But of a beautiful, unheard-of kind
> That is not in the world.
> . . . .
> Yet never have two lovers kissed but they
> Believed there was some other near at hand,
> And almost wept because they could not find it.

The rich music of the last lines of the play is one of the most
splendid of all expressions of this ideal of romantic love:

> You and I
> Shall be alone for ever. We two—this crown—
> I half remember. It has been in my dreams.
> Bend lower, O king, that I may crown you with it.
> O flower of the branch, O bird among the leaves,
> O silver fish that my live hands have taken
> Out of the running stream, O morning star,
> Trembling in the blue heavens like a white fawn
> Upon the misty border of the wood,
> Bend lower, that I may cover you with my hair,
> For we will gaze upon the world no longer.

The Shadowy Waters is the culmination of Yeat's symbolist poetry.
Reading Mallarmé many years later he wrote 'this was the road
I and others of my time went for certain furlongs. . . . It is not
the way I go now but one of the legitimate roads'. Some of the
poems in the collection called *In the Seven Woods* (1904) are still
in the symbolist manner but in one at least there is a new note of
sharp satire and realism:

> Better go down upon your marrow bones
> And scrub a kitchen pavement, or break stones
> Like an old pauper in all kinds of weather;
> For to articulate sweet sounds together
> Is to work harder than all these, and yet
> Be thought an idler by the noisy set
> Of bankers, schoolmasters, and clergymen
> The martyrs call the world.

At the end of the collection Yeats placed the remarkable poem

called 'The Happy Townland', which might be called his farewell
to symbolism. In one sense of the term he always remained a
symbolist, but the symbolism of the school of Mallarmé was too
inhuman a doctrine to provide a permanent home for his rich and
vital personality. In 'The Happy Townland' he uses the popular
Irish myth of a faery world of ideal happiness where men are freed
from the cares of material existence, but now instead of con-
ceiving it in the vague misty manner of his early poem, he paints
it in sharp, brilliant colours and concrete forms:

> Boughs have their fruit and blossom
> At all times of the year;
> Rivers are running over
> With red beer and brown beer.
> An old man plays the bagpipes
> In a gold and silver wood;
> Queens, their eyes blue like ice,
> Are dancing in a crowd.

The happy townland is a place of danger as well as beauty and
the traveller is warned:

> The little fox he murmured,
> 'O what of the world's bane?'
> The sun was laughing sweetly,
> The moon plucked at my rein;
> But the little red fox murmured,
> 'O do not pluck at his rein,
> He is riding to the townland
> That is the world's bane'.

This poem is a turning point in Yeats's development. He had
made the 'voyage within' and had discovered the beauty of the
'inner life', but he had also discovered that it was a terrible,
inhuman beauty . . . 'the world's bane'. This discovery made him
the master and not the servant of the terror.

After Yeats had made his great exploration of the inner life
under the guidance of the Symbolists, circumstances enabled him
to make the 'voyage without' in the stimulating atmosphere of
Dublin in the opening years of the twentieth century, the Dublin
of Mr Bloom and James Joyce's youth, of the Gaelic League and
the early days of Sinn Fein and above all of the Abbey Theatre and
the Irish literary movement of which he was the acknowledged

leader. The aesthetic recluse of the Rhymers' Club, the student
of the occult and adept of the Order of the Golden Dawn, the
guest of Lady Gregory at Coole, now became a public figure in
Dublin, dramatist, orator, wit and conversationalist. He was the
driving force behind the great experiment of the literary theatre,
directing rehearsals, organising performances and championing
his friend Synge against the attacks of bigoted nationalists and
puritanical Catholics who were shocked by his ironic and realistic
pictures of Irish peasant life. Sir Hugh Lane had offered his great
collection of modern paintings to Dublin on condition that the
Dublin Corporation would build a suitable gallery to house them.
Yeats used all his energy to support this proposal and to answer
the objections of philistines in both the nationalist and the unionist
camps.

The genius of Synge made an enormous impression on Yeats at
this time. The younger writer's 'harsh, heroical, clean, windswept
view of things' was exactly the stimulant that was needed by a
poet who was growing weary of romantic idealism and the
inhumanity of symbolist doctrine. The fullest expression of Synge's
genius is, of course, to be found in his plays, but his handful of short
poems must be reckoned as an important contribution to the poetry
of the modern crisis. Synge believed that contemporary poetry was
vitiated by confining itself to 'poetic' material, using the word
'poetic' in the same sense in which it is used in the phrase 'poetic
diction'. He pointed out that 'the older poets such as Villon,
Herrick and Burns who used the whole of their personal life as their
material' wrote 'verse . . . which was read by strong men, and
thieves and deacons, and not by little cliques only'. His verdict on
the condition of English poetry in his time was remarkably far-
sighted: 'It may almost be said that before verse can be human
again it must learn to be brutal'. His own poems are expressions
of brutal facts in language of savage simplicity, which is transformed into poetry by the intensity of his passion:

> I asked if I got sick and died, would you
> With my black funeral go walking too,
> If you'd stand close to hear them talk or pray
> While I'm let down in that steep bank of clay.
>
> And, No, you said, for if you saw that crew
> Of living idiots pressing round that new
> Oak coffin—they alive, I dead beneath
> That board—you'd rave and rend them with your teeth.

Nothing could be more unlike Yeats's early poems about 'white beauty', 'pearl pale hands' and 'cloud-pale eyelids'.

During the first six years of the twentieth century Yeats worked hard at writing plays for the Abbey Theatre. These plays were part of the means by which he was trying to create a new 'unity of life' for the whole Irish people based on their traditional heroic legends. The best of them are the two fine tragedies, *On Baile's Strand* (1904) and *Deirdre* (1906). Unlike *The Shadowy Waters* and even *The Countess Cathleen* they are essentially acting plays written for the stage by a poet who is also a man of the theatre. Yeats was too subjective and too lyrical to be a great dramatist yet he had a passion for the theatre and never ceased from experimenting in the drama up to the end of his career. To make plays that would act well he had to write clearly and concisely and to discipline his imagination by constructing shapely and effective plots. The clarity and directness of the speeches in these plays is very different from the romantic vagueness of his earlier work:

> You mean that when a man who has loved like that
> Is after crossed, love drowns in its own flood,
> And that love drowned and floating is but hate;
> And that a king who hates, sleeps ill at night,
> Till he has killed, and that, though the day laughs,
> We shall be dead at cock-crow.

In spite of their great merits, these plays suffer from the fact that they are built on an illusion. Yeats believed when he wrote them that by using the Gaelic legends he could 'bring the old folk life to Dublin . . . and with the folk life all the life of the heart.' In other words he thought he could create an audience like the audience of Shakespeare or Sophocles in twentieth-century Dublin. Actually, the legendary material, whatever it may have been among the peasants in Galway or Kerry, was mere antiquarianism in the Dublin of Mr Bloom. For Yeats himself the world of the old Irish sagas was a dream world providing a refuge from the ugliness of contemporary life.[1] This is not the material out of which great drama can be made. All Yeats's plans seemed to have failed in the years immediately preceding the First World War. Synge had died, an unhappy and disappointed man. The Abbey Theatre gave up the attempt to become the ideal 'People's Theatre' of his

---

[1] See Dorothy Hoare's *The Works of Morris and Yeats in Relation to Early Saga Literature* for an acute analysis of the difference between Yeats's attitude towards the Gaelic legends and that of the ancient Irish storytellers.

dreams, and under the management of Lennox Robinson concerned itself chiefly with realistic plays, 'objective with the
objectivity of the office and the workshop, of the newspaper and
the street, of mechanism and of politics'. Finally, after a bitter
struggle the Dublin Corporation rejected Sir Hugh Lane's pro-
posals for a great Irish Gallery of Modern Art. Some of Yeats's
contemporaries thought his literary career was at an end. Actually
the most important phase of it was only just beginning. Like
Dante and Milton he only started to write his greatest poetry when
all his projects in the sphere of action had ended in complete
disaster.

The beginning of the new Yeats is to be found in the poems
published with *The Green Helmet* in 1910. From these poems the
romantic decoration, the mythology and the vague incantatory
music of his earlier works have been almost entirely banished. In
their place there is terse, unadorned language and rhythms of an
almost Wordsworthian simplicity. The emotion communicated by
Yeats's earlier lyrics is nearly always vague and remote. In the
poems published with *The Green Helmet* there is a new immediacy
and concreteness. For instance the poem called 'No Second Troy',
unlike the early poems on Maud Gonne, makes the reader share
not a vague general emotion but a particular experience:

> Why should I blame her that she filled my days
> With misery, or that she would of late
> Have taught to ignorant men most violent ways,
> Or hurled the little streets upon the great,
> Had they but courage equal to desire?
> What could have made her peaceful with a mind
> That nobleness made simple as a fire,
> With beauty like a tightened bow, a kind
> That is not natural in an age like this,
> Being high and solitary and most stern?
> Why, what could she have done, being what she is?
> Was there another Troy for her to burn?

The fourth line of this poem illustrates the new concreteness of
this phase of Yeats's poetry and also a new power of including in
poetic experience material from daily life which had hitherto
been avoided. The poem is not a contemplation of abstract love
but a successful attempt to show what it is like to love a particular
beautiful woman who is also a political agitator.

The turning point in Yeats's development was the publication

of the volume of poems called *Responsibilities* in 1914. In these
poems he widens the scope of his subject matter to include ironic
commentary on contemporary affairs. The splendid elegy on
O'Leary is poetry made out of the stuff of contemporary life, and
of the poet's contempt for its sordid spirit of money-grubbing:

> What need you, being come to sense,
> But fumble in a greasy till
> And add the halfpence to the pence
> And prayer to shivering prayer, until
> You have dried the marrow from the bone?
> For men were born to pray and save:
> Romantic Ireland's dead and gone,
> It's with O'Leary in the grave.

Now instead of the remote mythology of Gaelic legend he creates
a new mythology out of the memory of the patriots of eighteenth-
century Ireland who still lived in the popular imagination:

> Was it for this the wild geese spread
> The grey wing upon every tide;
> For this that all that blood was shed,
> For this Edward Fitzgerald died,
> And Robert Emmet and Wolfe Tone,
> All that delirium of the brave?

Here the language is that of common speech but, as in Synge's
poems, it is ennobled by sheer intensity of passion. Yeats has come
out of the ivory tower of symbolism, but he has brought with
him a power capable of transforming contemporary actualities into
the material of high poetry. The poem called 'A Coat' is at once a
searching self-criticism and a manifesto of a new art which would
no longer evade actualities:

> I made my song a coat
> Covered with embroideries
> Out of old mythologies
> From heel to throat;
> But the fools caught it,
> Wore it in the world's eyes
> As though they'd wrought it.
> Song, let them take it,
> For there's more enterprise
> In walking naked.

Yeats was in Dublin at the time of the rebellion of Easter 1916. He was deeply moved by the heroism and the martyrdom of the insurgents. He had little sympathy with their political methods, but with a true poet's insight he saw that the whole Irish scene was transformed by the tragedy of their execution. Now he no longer writes of contemporary Ireland with scorn or irony but of the common life of Dublin irradiated by the magnificence of tragedy:

> I have met them at close of day
> Coming with vivid faces
> From counter or desk among grey
> Eighteenth century houses.
> I have passed with a nod of the head
> Or polite meaningless words.
> Or have lingered awhile and said
> Polite meaningless words,
> And thought before I had done
> Of a mocking tale or a gibe
> To please a companion
> Around the fire at the club,
> Being certain that they and I
> But lived where motley is worn:
> All changed, changed utterly;
> A terrible beauty is born.

The heroes of the rebellion, Pearse, Connolly, Macdonagh and Macbride, now became symbols of heroic martyrdom, and Yeats, perhaps alone among modern English-speaking poets, succeeds in creating a truly poetical myth out of contemporary politics. To celebrate them he used with remarkable success the form of the Dublin street ballad, a kind of popular poetry which was still alive in the twentieth century. The ballad called 'The Rose Tree' is a terse dialogue between Pearse and Connolly in which the movement of the street ballad and its simple imagery are raised to the level of high poetry. The 'rose tree' is dying for lack of water. It is withered, perhaps, by 'a breath of politic words' or 'a wind that blows across the bitter sea'. Connolly tells Pearse how it can be made to bloom again:

> 'But where can we draw water,'
>   Said Pearse to Connolly,
> 'When all the wells are parched away?
>   O plain as plain can be
> There's nothing but our own red blood
>   Can make a right Rose Tree.'

The rose, which in Yeats's early poems was a symbol of an unattainable dream world has now become a symbol of a living political idealism. Yeats's political poems are not magical incantations or exorcisms like Kipling's. They are sane, clear-eyed and unsentimental. He is not afraid to call one of the martyrs 'a drunken vainglorious lout'. He even suggests that their death may after all be 'needless', 'For England may keep faith'. It is the moderation and sanity which gives such tremendous power to his celebration of the heroism of the men who died in April, 1916.

Yeat's most memorable and important poetry was not written till he was over fifty. It is to be found in the series of volumes which he published in the years immediately following the end of the First World War: *The Wild Swans at Coole* (1919), *Michael Robartes and The Dancer* (1921), *The Tower* (1928) and *The Winding Stair* (1933). In these years he was reading widely in the philosophers, Plato, Plotinus, Vico, Hegel, Croce and Whitehead, and he was particularly impressed by the idealism of George Berkeley, the Irish eighteenth-century bishop, 'God-appointed Berkeley that proved all things a dream'. From about 1920 onwards he was working out the curious and elaborate system of occult thought which he expounded in the prose work called *A Vision* (1925). The lady whom he had married in 1916 was a medium and with her he had conducted various experiments in spiritualism. He could not be content with the illogical dualism of the average modern man who accepts scientific naturalism with one part of his mind and belief in a divinely revealed religion with the other. On the other hand he could not accept the traditional Christian theology. As he himself wrote, he had an essentially religious mind; his mind was also orderly and logical. So, like William Blake, he constructed a system of belief out of his own private experiences. This is the system of *A Vision*, a doctrine of reincarnation, according to which all the types of humanity are arranged in a cycle or 'great wheel' consisting of twenty-eight phases corresponding to the phases of the moon. Every soul has to pass through these twenty-eight phases and history is simply a cyclic repetition of the phases of the 'great wheel'. The system is further complicated by the division of each soul into four 'faculties': 'will', 'mask', 'creative mind' and 'body of fate'. It is strange to find Yeats elaborating this fanciful yet inhuman and abstract system of determinism accompanied by various romantic mystifications at the very time when his personality was acquiring an unrivalled richness and power through a new vital contact with humanity and the contemporary world. He himself was fond of quoting Goethe's saying that 'a poet cannot have too much philosophy but he ought to keep it out of his poetry'. Yeats did not keep the 'philosophy' of *A Vision* out of all his later poems, but those in which he used it directly such as 'Ego Dominus Tuus', 'The Phases of the Moon' and 'The Double Vision of Michael Robartes', in spite of notable passages, are artistic failures. The 'philosophy' seems to have been chiefly valuable not as the material for poetry but as a kind of map of the inner life, a spiritual framework like that which Catholicism provided for Hopkins. The power and intensity of the best poems in his later volumes was certainly due to a synthesis of a realistic and humorous view of life with the strengthened visionary power arising from his occult adventures. Soon after the first version of *A Vision* was published he wrote of it as something which he had to get out of his system before the poetry he wanted to write would be possible: 'I have not . . . dealt with the whole of my subject . . . but I am longing to put it out of my reach that I may write the poetry it seems to have made possible. I can now, if I have the energy, find the simplicity I have sought in vain. I need no longer write poems like "The Phases of the Moon". . . . Nor spend years . . . striving with abstractions'. *A Vision* did not provide a new mythology for Yeats's later poetry but it provided a background which illuminates the dynamic myths of his maturity with a visionary radiance.

In this poetry the vague figures of Celtic legend and the tragic heroes of 1916 are replaced partly by the great men of Protestant eighteenth-century Ireland, Swift and Berkeley, Goldsmith and Burke, partly by the figures who had played a significant part in Yeats's own experience, Lionel Johnson, 'that loved his learning better than mankind', 'that enquiring man John Synge' and 'old George Pollexfen, in muscular youth well known to Mayo men'. Yeats remained a symbolist in his later poetry but he now moved to a far wider and deeper conception of symbolism, which was his interpretation of Platonic idealism particularly in the form in which it was restated by Berkeley. He now saw the whole material world as a symbolic dramatisation of eternity and he was free to choose his symbols from the whole range of his reading and personal experience. Two of the most impressive are Byzantium, the holy city, which is at once an idealised Ireland and a timeless paradise, and the image of himself as a terrible and dynamic old man for whom old age is not decrepitude but a spiritual adventure. This is the old poet of 'Sailing to Byzantium', a poem where he achieves a true 'unity of life', 'an organic thing . . . the flow of

flesh under the impulse of passionate thought'. The subject of this
poem is really the same as that of 'The Song of Wandering Aengus'
and *The Shadowy Waters*, the quest for a timeless existence transcending the world of sensuous experience. But now this theme is
embodied not in the vaguely beautiful symbols of romantic love
but in images which (to use Ben Jonson's phrase that Yeats was
fond of quoting) are 'ramm'd with life':

> That is no country for old men. The young
> In one another's arms, birds in the trees
> —Those dying generations—at their song,
> The salmon-falls, the mackerel-crowded seas,
> Fish, flesh, or fowl, commend all summer long
> Whatever is begotten, born and dies.
> Caught in that sensual music all neglect
> Monuments of unageing intellect.

Against this 'richly concrete evocation of instinctive life'[1] the
figure of the old poet is seen, at once slightly ridiculous and yet
frightening:

> An aged man is but a paltry thing,
> A tattered coat upon a stick, unless
> Soul clap its hand and sing, and louder sing
> For every tatter in its mortal dress,
> Nor is there singing school but studying
> Monuments of its own magnificence;
> And therefore I have sailed the seas and come
> To the holy city of Byzantium.

In the 'Song of Wandering Aengus' the poet's imagination is
not capacious enough to include laughter. In 'Sailing to Byzantium'
he can laugh at the absurdity of the scarecrow body of the old man
and yet retain his dignity and seriousness. The laughter is drowned
in the noble music that announces the voyage to the 'holy city of
Byzantium', no dim wraith like the 'glimmering girl' of the
earlier poem but the concrete splendour of the Byzantine mosaic
representing a timeless world that lives with a life more intense
than that of the 'dying generations' of the first stanza:

> O sages standing in God's holy fire
> As in the gold mosaic of a wall,

---

[1] The phrase is that of L. C. Knights in his fine essay on Yeats in *Explorations*.

> Come from the holy fire, perne in a gyre,
> And be the singing masters of my soul.
> Consume my heart away; sick with desire
> And fastened to a dying animal
> It knows not what it is; and gather me
> Into the artifice of eternity.

'Sailing to Byzantium' (1920) should be read in conjunction with its sequel, 'Byzantium', written four years later. The first poem is a picture of a voyage from the material world to the holy city of eternity; the second is a vision of the city from the inside where the soul is imaged first as a walking mummy and then as the Emperor's golden bird, whose 'glory of changeless metal' is contrasted with the 'complexities of mire and blood'. Here Byzantium is a Purgatory as well as a Paradise, a place of cleansing flames:

> Flames that no faggot feeds, nor steel has lit,
> Nor storm disturbs, flames begotten of flame.

'Sailing to Byzantium' is a meditation on timeless existence or eternity. 'Among Schoolchildren', the other great achievement of Yeats's maturity, is a meditation on existence in time, the world of becoming. As 'Sailing to Byzantium' can be related to 'The Song of Wandering Aengus', 'Among schoolchildren' can be related to the early poems on Maud Gonne such as 'When you are old' (see above, p. 80). In that poem Yeats, following Ronsard, had imagined his mistress in old age sitting by the fire and remembering his love, and had then allowed his mood of vague desire to lead him to the sentimental image of Love on the mountains hiding his face 'amid a crowd of stars'. In 'Among Schoolchildren' he starts with a vivid picture of himself as an elderly Senator of the Irish Free State inspecting a convent school. Again there is ironic humour both in the glimpse of the education of the children and in the self-portrait:

> I walk through the long schoolroom questioning,
> A kind old nun in a white hood replies;
> The children learn to cipher and to sing,
> To study reading-books and histories,
> To cut and sew, be neat in everything
> In the best modern way—the children's eyes
> In momentary wonder stare upon
> A sixty year old smiling public man.

D

The sight of the girls recalls Maud Gonne, not imagined in a vague romantic old age, but as she actually was when, 'bent above a sinking fire', she told the poet of 'a harsh reproof or trivial event, that changed some childish day to tragedy',

> Told, and it seemed that our two natures blent
> Into a sphere from youthful sympathy,
> Or else, to alter Plato's parable,
> Into the yolk and white of the one shell.

The ageing Maud Gonne is no mere fantasy but a living woman whose fading beauty is contrasted with the freshness of childhood:

> Her present image floats into the mind—
> Did Quattrocento finger fashion it
> Hollow of cheek as though it drank the wind
> And took a mess of shadows for its meat?

Beside the pathos of this portrait is set the mockery of the old poet in his official mask of respectability:

> Better to smile on all that smile, and show
> There is a comfortable kind of old scarecrow.

This record of personal experience is the prelude to a series of questionings on the mystery of life. First there is the paradox of the suffering of the mother in travail for 'a shape upon her lap' which must turn at last into the 'comfortable kind of old scarecrow', 'that shape with sixty or more winters on its head'. Then the theories of the philosophers are set forth in dancing lyrical music and dismissed with flashing wit:

> Plato thought nature but a spume that plays
> Upon a ghostly paradigm of things;
> Solider Aristotle played the taws
> Upon the bottom of a king of kings;
> World-famous golden-thighed Pythagoras
> Fingered upon a fiddle-stick or strings
> What a star sang and careless Muses heard:
> Old clothes upon old sticks to scare a bird.

Finally the nuns like the mothers are shown worshipping images, though theirs are lit by candles and 'keep a marble or a bronze

repose'. These 'presences' symbolize 'all heavenly glory' and yet
they too are:

> Self-born mockers of man's enterprise.

The last stanza answers all the questionings by showing a beauty
which is perpetual growth and movement, the wholeness of life
which defies analysis:

> Labour is blossoming or dancing where
> The body is not bruised to pleasure soul,
> Nor beauty born out of its own despair,
> Nor blear-eyed wisdom out of midnight oil,
> O chestnut-tree, great rooted blossomer,
> Are you the leaf, the blossom or the bole?
> O body swayed to music, O brightening glance,
> How can we know the dancer from the dance?

This is poetry in which the outer and inner lives are brought
together in a unity which includes realism, wit, lyrical beauty and
philosophic meditation. It is not a synthesis in which we feel a
sense of terrible effort and strain as we do in much of the best work
of Hopkins, but it seems to arise easily and naturally from the
poet's mind

> as the leaves grow on the tree.

In a few great poems Yeats achieved this triumphant wholeness of
poetic life. His great ambition of creating a 'unity of life' for the
whole Irish nation was shattered by the vulgarity and insensitive-
ness of the modern world. In his old age he gloried in being un-
popular, identifying himself deliberately with aristocracy and
wealth, the life of the great country houses—which was indeed
little more than an empty memory in the twentieth century—and
flirting with fascism, which he seems at first to have mistaken for
the beginning of a new aristocratic civilisation. He had, he writes,
a conception that had freed him 'from British Liberalism and all its
dreams', but he was never completely emancipated from nineteenth-century romanticism in spite of his rejection of romantic
diction and romantic imagery. In his early poems he uses the
vague and beautiful images of flowers, stars, birds and mythical
figures as an escape from the ugliness of his age. In his later poetry
he uses the more realistic images of drunkards and lechers, Crazy

Jane and Tom the Lunatic, and finally the figure of the mad reckless old poet in that splendid piece of bravado, 'The Statesman's Holiday':

> With boys and girls about him,
>   With any sort of clothes,
> With a hat out of fashion,
>   With old patched shoes,
> With a ragged bandit cloak,
>   With an eye like a hawk,
> With a stiff straight back,
>   With a strutting turkey walk. . . .

There is much more vitality here than in the poetry of the Celtic Twilight, but it is really only another kind of defiant protest against that ugliness and vulgarity which Yeats called Whiggery:

> A levelling, rancorous, rational sort of mind
> That never looked out of the eye of a saint
> Or out of drunkard's eye.

Both are the work of an isolated and therefore incomplete genius, and, in this sense, Yeats's work, like that of Hopkins, if judged by the highest standards, can be called, as L. C. Knights has called it, 'a heroic failure'. Yeats himself, a most penetrating critic, was quite aware of his limitations. 'All my life', he wrote in his *Diary kept in 1909*, 'I have been haunted with the idea that the poet should know all classes of men as one of themselves, that he should combine the greatest possible personal realisation with the greatest possible knowledge of the speech and circumstances of the world. . . . But when one shrinks from all business with a stranger, and is unnatural with all who are not intimate friends, because one underrates or overrates unknown people, one cannot adventure forth. The artist grows more and more distinct, more and more a being in his own right as it were, but more and more loses grasp of the always more complex world'. Like Hopkins he succeeded in overcoming the modern crisis by means of an integration of his own personality but he only achieved that integration at the expense of 'losing grasp of the always more complex world'. This consciousness of failure to achieve that larger 'unity of life' of which he had dreamed lends a strange pathos to the noble epitaph which he composed for himself:

> Cast a cold eye
> On life, on death.
> Horseman, pass by.

5

EDWARDIANS AND GEORGIANS

At the opening of the twentieth century English society as it had existed since the age of the Tudors was in a state of disintegration. For four hundred years, as C. F. G. Masterman wrote, 'the essential England had been the English countryside, "the rich man in his castle, the poor man at his gate" ... the feudal society of country house, country village and little country town in a land whose immense wealth slept undisturbed'. 'No one', continues the same writer, 'today [i.e. 1908] would seek in the ruined villages and dwindling population of the countryside the spirit of an England, four-fifths of whose people have now crowded into cities. The little red-roofed towns and hamlets, the labourer in the fields at noontide or evening, the old English service in the old English village church, now stand but as the historical survival of a once great and splendid past'. This old England had three classes, the aristocracy, the middle class and the working class, each with its distinctive cultural tradition. When it was functioning healthily, each of these traditions was alive and creative. Courtiers wrote sonnets, love lyrics, romances and sometimes plays, the middle class produced first the drama and then the novel besides a great body of serious poetry and prose, and the peasants and labourers had their ballads and songs. Each of the traditions was strengthened by contact with the others. The eighteenth-century novel of Fielding and Sterne and 'bourgeois' poetry from Spenser and Milton to Wordsworth and Tennyson were profoundly influenced by aristocratic ideals on the one hand and were never wholly out of touch with the popular tradition on the other. Finally there was a religious tradition which was not the property of any class and could be shared by the aristocrat George Herbert, the tinker John Bunyan and the typical middle-class divine Isaac Watts. The industrial revolution during the nineteenth century had destroyed both the aristocratic and the popular traditions of culture. Byron was the last great English literary aristocrat and by the middle of the century the aristocracy was becoming culturally absorbed by the middle class. The popular tradition lingered on well into the century, but after about 1880 only survived in odd corners of Britain.

In the new England of the twentieth century there were new classes without any tradition of culture. There were the new rich, 'the most unpremeditated, successful, aimless, plutocracy that ever cumbered the destinies of mankind'. 'It maintains large country houses which offer a lavish hospitality', writes Masterman, 'but it sees rural England crumbling into ruin just outside their boundaries. . . . It fills vast hotels scattered round the coasts of England, and ever multiplying in the capital. . . . It has annexed whole regions abroad, Biarritz and the Riviera coast, Austrian and German watering places. . . . At the best it is an existence with some boredom in it. . . . At its worst it becomes a nightmare and a delirium'. These people, unlike the 'new rich' of the sixteenth century, failed to continue and develop the culture bequeathed to them by their predecessors. The new 'rich man in his castle' might give great benefactions to a hospital or even to a university, but he had no great library and no poets, artists or philosophers in his train. Already in the eighteenth century Hume had observed the rise of this new kind of plutocrat: 'If the employment you give him be lucrative, especially if the profit be attached to every particular exertion of industry, he has gains so often in his eye, that he acquires by degrees a passion for it, and knows no such pleasure as that of seeing the daily increase of his fortune'. In the nineteenth century the development of this sort of human profit-making machine was checked to some extent by living traditions of culture. At the opening of the twentieth these traditions were mostly dead, and the men who controlled the vast wealth produced by industry had for the most part the outlook on the arts summarised by May Sinclair's Dicky Pilkington. 'Dicky had arrived at the inspired moment of the evening, and was chanting the hymn of Finance. "Look", said Dicky, "at the Power it gives you. Now all you writing chaps, you're not in it at all. You're simply 'opping and dodging round the outside—you 'aven't a chance of really seeing the show.

Whereas—look at me. I go and take my seat plump down in the middle of the stage-box. I've got my 'ear to the heart of 'umanity and my hand on its pulse. I've got a grip of realities. You say you want to por-tray life. Very well por-tray it. When all's said and done you've only got a picture. And wot's the picture, if it's ever so life-like? You 'aven't got a bit nearer to the real thing. I tell you, you aren't in it with me".[1]

For one kind of rich man of this period the 'life' of Dicky Pilkington was 'bridge and women and champagne'; for another it was the 'simple life' of G. K. Chesterton's Good Rich Man:—

Mr Mandragon, the Millionaire, he wouldn't have wine or wife,
He couldn't endure complexity: he lived the Simple Life.
He ordered his lunch by megaphone in manly, simple tones,
And used all his motors for canvassing voters, and twenty telephones.

Even for the best of them, those who collected works of art like Henry James's Mr Verver, or bought Italian palaces like his Milly Theale, there was a curse on their money. They seemed to live in a hollow, empty world 'befogged with the stupidity which hangs over this society and prevents them from using their money rationally'. They lived behind what Henry James called 'an impenetrable ring-fence within which reigned a kind of expensive vagueness made up of smiles and silences and beautiful fictions and priceless arrangements, all strained to breaking'.

At the other end of the social scale there were the horrors of the English slums, still, in the reign of Edward VII, in spite of all the efforts of government officials and philanthropists, among the most sordid and brutal places in Europe. This is the world of Arthur Morrison's *Tales of Mean Streets* and *Children of the Jago*, of George Gissing's Litany Lane in *The Unclassed* and of Charles Booth's *Life and Labour in London*, a world of dark courts, broken glass, rags, bones and soul-destroying poverty. It is the world revealed by the Report of H.M. Factory Inspectors published in 1907, who found 'five beds infested with bugs in one room', and of the Medical Officer of Health of the same period who described forty little girls whom he found licking adhesive labels by the mouth at thirty gross a day, 'whose tongues had the polished tip characteristic of gum-lickers and the rest of the tongue coated coated with brown gum'.

[1] May Sinclair, *The Divine Fire* (1904), p. 245.

Just above this world was that of the great class of manual workers in more or less steady employment, yet always in danger of sinking into the festering poverty of the slums,[1] 'the enormous sea of persons, a multitude of cloth caps and shapeless clothing and little white faces' seen by an onlooker at one of Will Crooks's meetings outside the gates of Woolwich Arsenal in the reign of Edward VII. Among these people only the faintest relics of the old tradition of popular ballad poetry lingered in a few pathetic broadsides like that sold in the streets at the funeral of Edward VII:

> Heavenly Father, help in sorrow
> Queen-Mother, and them to follow,
> How to do without him who is gone
> Pray help, help, and do lead us on.
>
> Greatest sorrow England ever had
> When death took away our dear Dad.
> A king he was from head to sole,
> Beloved by his people one and all.
>
> His mighty work for the nation
> Strengthening peace and securing union,
> Always at it since on the throne
> Has saved the country more than one billion.

The place that popular poetry and music had filled in the lives of the ancestors of the twentieth-century proletarians was now being taken by machine-made amusements, the Sunday newspaper, the music hall, the football match and a little later the cinema.

Between these two extremes was the vast area of the middle class stretching from the people who lived in large 'detached' villas with many servants, sending their children to public schools and Oxford or Cambridge, and taking their holidays on the Continent, to the great army of clerks and shop-assistants, whose lot was often far less enviable than that of the skilled manual worker. These were the inhabitants of the suburbs which had grown up and were continuing to spread for miles round London and other great cities, the rows of smaller or larger villas inhabited by white-collared black-coated men who worked daily in shops and offices 'adding up other men's accounts and writing other men's letters' and selling other men's goods. On Sundays they worshipped in neo-Gothic

---

[1] It must be remembered that at this date there was no unemployment pay or National Insurance.

churches built by Butterfield and similar architects but their real gods were security and respectability. This class included the most complacent and reactionary part of the population, Galsworthy's 'island pharisees' who opposed every political and social reform and were implacably hostile to any new or vital development in art or literature. 'Suburban villadom', wrote L. T. Hobhouse,[1] 'is a political and social portent the meaning of which has never yet been fully analysed. All round every great centre is a ring of towns to which the men resort only to dine and sleep, while the women have no visible function in life except to marry and discuss marriages. While the private life of the suburb is no doubt comfortable and blameless it is a greater burden on the nation than the slum. It has, to begin with, no healthy corporate life. Its menfolk are engaged elsewhere and are too much exhausted by their own business to enter into public life, or they are retired officers and civilians, residents whose only function is to reside. We have a class of moderately well-to-do people almost wholly divorced from definite public duties—a class relatively new in this country. They are removed from contact with poverty or from any special obligation to any class of dependants. All they know of social and domestic reform is that it means expense, and their politics are summed up in the simple and comprehensive formula—keep down the rates. Imperialism is the only conception remotely related to an ideal which they comprehend, and, if this is too expensive, we have seen that it offers them as a class ample compensation'. These people, the 'big battalions of suburbia', as Hobhouse calls them, were not the whole of the middle class by any means but they formed a very substantial part of it and their mentality infected the whole intellectual climate of the time. They had literary traditions, but especially in the field of poetry, these were overlaid by a thick veneer of a conservatism that was at once academic and puritanical. Poetry was regarded as something inseparable from the worship of the classics, and especially the Victorian classics, Tennyson, Browning and Arnold. Kipling was an exception, but he was tolerated because of his imperialist politics, though his best verse was regarded as rather vulgar and not 'poetry'. Poetry had to be pleasant, dignified, moral, not difficult or introspective, and based on the pretence that the rhythms of suburban life were still those of the old England of the feudal countryside. It was the poetry of the school-prize bound in half-morocco. Sir William Watson

---

[1] In *Democracy and Reaction* (1909), p. 70.

(1858-1935) was the typical poet of educated suburbia at the opening
of the twentieth century, a poet for headmasters, clergymen and
others educated at the public schools and old universities, the
world of E. M. Forster's Sawston in *The Longest Journey*.
Watson wrote polished and melodious elegies on Tennyson and
Matthew Arnold and an 'Ode on the Coronation of Edward VII':

> Sire, we have looked on many and mighty things
> In these eight hundred summers of renown.
> Since the Gold Dragon of the Wessex Kings
> On Hastings field went down;
> And slowly in the ambience of this crown
> Have many crowns been gathered, till to-day,
> How many peoples crown thee, who shall say?
>
> Time and the ocean and some fostering star,
> In high cabal have made us what we are,
> Who stretch one hand on Huron's bearded pines,
> And one on Kashmir's snowy shoulders lay,
> And round the streaming of whose raiment shines
> The iris of the Australasian spray.

In spite of its technical dexterity this is verse written in a dead
language and in rhythms that bear no relation to those of contemporary English life. The language comes from the study of Tennyson, Arnold and Milton and it has no contact with the speech that
the Edwardians used in their streets, their public houses or even
their drawing rooms and libraries. Nor has it the vitality of a
literary diction that derives its origin from an enthusiasm for a
great tradition. To use the phrase which Henry James applied to
the lives of the rich in this period, it has a kind of 'expensive
vagueness' and its echoes of the English classics are like samples of
vintages enjoyed by a wealthy connoisseur. Its rhythms are those
of the dying agricultural England, not the contemporary England
of the internal combustion engine, the express train and the factory.
    Nevertheless the 'big battalions of suburbia' were not the
whole of the middle class. There was still a considerable part of
this class which retained the cultural traditions of nineteenth-
century families like the Ruskins and Brownings, and was alive
to the necessity for change and development both in politics and
in literature. There were 'the more thoughtful of the middle class'
which L. T. Hobhouse[1] noted in 1904 together with the 'artisans'

---

[1] L. T. Hobhouse, *Democracy and Reaction*, pp. 69, 70.

as being 'aroused to a sense of public danger and to a fuller compre-
hension of the drift of the reaction'. These people had some
apprehension of the true nature of the transformation of English
society which was taking place and of the means by which a new
civilisation could be built. The more intelligent among them
could see that, to survive, English civilisation had to transcend the
limitations of class and nationality and build up a 'great society'
led by an *élite* instead of a series of unrelated 'small societies' consisting of decayed relics of an old class system which could not
function properly in the modern world. The Boer War, which
ended in 1902, had opened the eyes of Englishmen to the bankruptcy
of the commercialised imperialism of Joseph Chamberlain and his
friends, and the development of the Labour movement of Keir
Hardie and Will Crooks revealed the condition of the 'submerged
tenth', the 'prisoners' who rotted in the hold of modern capitalism
while saloon passengers were enjoying 'beautiful fictions and priceless arrangements' on deck. A new liberalism far more sympathetic
to social reform and even to 'socialism' than the old Gladstonian
brand spread rapidly among the intelligent part of the middle
class, and was preached by such teachers and writers as G. Lowes
Dickinson, C. F. G. Masterman and L. T. Hobhouse. The collapse
of the Conservative government in 1905 and the sweeping Liberal-
Labour victory at the General Election of 1906 gave the new
liberalism a chance to succeed where the old liberalism had failed.
The two great tasks which lay before it were the replacement of
the old authoritarian empire by a free commonwealth of nations,
involving the granting of self-government to Ireland, South Africa
and India, and the removal of the festering sores of poverty and
unemployment by means of sweeping reforms on 'socialist' lines
based on a more equitable system of taxation. The new liberalism
embodied in the Campbell-Bannerman and Asquith governments
made determined and partly successful efforts to carry out these
tasks and thus bring about a new harmony between the men of
vision and the men of action.[1] Unfortunately these efforts were
hampered not only by the opposition of nearly all the 'moneyed
interests' in England but also by the growing threat of German
imperialism which had to be answered by the piling up of armaments
on the physical plane, and on the intellectual, by the revival of that
very nationalism which it was the mission of the new liberalism
to destroy.

[1] See above p. 14.

The resurgence of liberal England was the political aspect of a spiritual awakening which found expression in a remarkable literary revival. Its great achievements were in the fields of prose fiction and drama rather than of poetry probably because these forms were less constrained than verse was by academic conservatism. The plays of Bernard Shaw, Granville Barker, Barrie, Galsworthy and St John Hankin and the novels of Wells, Arnold Bennett, Joseph Conrad and E. M. Forster were the notable literary achievements of the last great age of English liberalism.[1] It produced no new poet comparable with Hardy and Yeats (though some of their best work was done in this period) and no experimenter[2] in poetic technique to continue the work of G. M. Hopkins, which was still almost entirely unknown. Yet in the first decade of the twentieth century there was a real, though comparatively limited, revival of poetry. This was not the much trumpeted 'Georgian' movement which modern critics often mistakenly regard as the only development in English poetry between the late Victorians and T. S. Eliot. Actually the best poets of 'pre-war' twentieth-century England had all produced important work some years before the publication of the first volume of *Georgian Poetry*. They were G. K. Chesterton, Walter de la Mare, Lascelles Abercrombie, Edward Thomas, John Masefield and W. H. Davies.

G. K. Chesterton (1872–1936), the son of a London house agent, united the social morality of the new liberalism with a re-discovery of the values of traditional religion and a very English sense of the poetry of the absurd, the grotesque, and the fantastic and the illogical. He found a real literary inspiration in the suburbs seen from the angle of a romantic poet who could find beauty in sights like that of

> the great grey water-tower
> That strikes the stars on Campden Hill.

Chesterton's most successful attempts to make poetry out of this vision of the suburbs are perhaps to be found in his prose fantasies like *The Napoleon of Notting Hill* (1904) and *The Man Who Was Thursday* (1908). Much of his verse is too clever, too slick and too

---

[1] The following dates are significant: *Man and Superman* (1903), *Major Barbara* (1905), *Tono-Bungay* (1909), *The Old Wives' Tale* (1908), *The Voysey Inheritance* (1909), *Howards End* (1910).

[2] G. M. Doughty (1843–1926) is a possible exception, but the poetic genius of this great traveller and writer of English prose was stunted by his devotion to obsolete poetic forms and by his excessive reverence for antiquity.

obviously influenced by the swinging, blustering rhythms of Kipling, though these are a great deal better than the devitalised iambics of Sir William Watson and have a real relationship with the life of the age of the first motor 'buses and taxicabs. Chesterton's poetry is seen at its worst in the popular anthology piece 'Lepanto', which seems like an attempt to escape from the boredom of suburbia by putting on a gorgeous dress and clashing cymbals. Yet even in this somewhat meretricious piece of decoration there are lines that reveal his remarkable power of apprehending the significance of history and making poetry out of it:

> The cold queen of England is looking in the glass;
> The shadow of the Valois is yawning at the Mass.

In his best poems such as 'The Secret People' he, combines this historical sense with a penetrating criticism of contemporary society:

> We hear men speaking for us of new laws strong and sweet,
> Yet there is no man speaketh as we speak in the street.
> It may be we shall rise the last as Frenchmen rose the first,
> Our wrath come after Russia's wrath and our wrath be the worst.
> It may be we are meant to mark with our riot and our rest
> God's scorn for all men governing. It may be beer is best.
> But we are the people of England; and we have not spoken yet.
> Smile at us, pay us, pass us. But do not quite forget.

This poem seems to be written by a young Kipling miraculously reborn with his eyes open to the realities of the modern crisis.

Chesterton's 'Ballad of the White Horse' is, perhaps, the best attempt to revive the narrative ballad since 'The Ancient Mariner'. It has none of Coleridge's magic, but a gusty strength that sometimes passes into bluster and bravado. In some of his shorter poems Chesterton reveals the absurdity of the contemporary situation with a vision that is at once comic and imaginative in its devastating criticism:

> If I had been a Heathen,
>   I'd have crowned Neæra's curls.
> And filled my life with love affairs,
>   My house with dancing girls;
> But Higgins is a Heathen,
>   And to lecture rooms is forced,
> Where his aunts, who are not married,
>   Demand to be divorced.

If I had been a Heathen,
    I'd have sent my armies forth,
And dragged behind my chariots
    The Chieftains of the North.
But Higgins is a Heathen,
    And he drives the dreary quill,
To lend the poor that funny cash
    That makes them poorer still.

If Chesterton made a new 'voyage without' with a better ideological
equipment than Kipling's, Walter de la Mare (1873–1956), a
descendant of an old Huguenot family, who worked in a city
office from 1889 to 1909, made the most successful 'voyage within'
of any poet since Yeats. Entirely ignoring the experiments of the
French symbolists, he created a new poetry of the inner life derived
from the English tradition of the medieval ballads and popular
songs, Blake, Coleridge, the Keats of 'La Belle Dame Sans Merci',
Edgar Allan Poe and Christina Rossetti. To quote his own words,
he is one of 'the visionaries, the introverts, whose eyes are set
inward and who delight in the distance, in the beginning and the
end, rather than in the assaulting, external incidents and excite-
ments of life's journey'.[1] Except in a few early sonnets, the blank
verse 'Characters from Shakespeare' and a few other pieces, he
avoids the rhythms of the official Parnassian poetry of the upper
middle class and creates very subtle and suggestive verse forms
which derive from the 'sprung rhythms' of ballad, nursery rhyme
and folksong and which express the spiritual experience of his age
no less effectively than the clanging, scurrying metres of a Kipling
and a Chesterton express its restless, mechanised physical existence.
The bewilderment and despair of an age which had lost the traditional clues to the labyrinth of the inner life are already admirably
embodied (not stated) in a poem that appeared in De la Mare's
volume published in 1906:

'Who called?' I said, and the words
    Through the whispering glades,
Hither, thither, baffled the birds—
    'Who called? Who called?'

The leafy boughs on high
    Hissed in the sun;

[1] Essay on 'Rupert Brooke and the Intellectual Imagination' in *Pleasures and
Speculations*, p. 180.

The dark air carried my cry
   Faintingly on;—

Eyes in the green, in the shade,
   In the motionless brake,
Voices that said what I said,
   For mockery's sake;—

'Who calls?' I bawled thro' my tears;
   The wind fell low:
In the silence, 'Who cares? Who cares?'
   Wailed to and fro.

One part of De la Mare's achievement was the creation of a poetry of idealised childhood, a mythical world akin to that of Blake's *Songs of Innocence and Experience* and Christina Rossetti's 'Goblin Market'. This is the De la Mare of *Songs of Childhood* and *Peacock Pie*, a poet who successfully revived the tradition of the nursery rhyme and child poem, charging it with a strange imaginative intensity which did not exclude either humour or romantic horror. In the rhythms of nursery rhyme adapted by a master of metrical techniques he found a satisfying alternative both to the classic English metres and to the strident anapaests of the Swinburne-Kipling tradition:

I heard a horseman
   Ride over the hill;
The moon shone clear,
   The night was still;
His helm was silver
   And pale was he;
And the horse he rode
   Was of ivory.

Poems like this are perfect in their kind (as Chesterton's little satiric poems are in theirs), but it is a small and limited kind with a touch of the *pastiche* and the 'folk' revival in it.

The other De la Mare is a much more important poet. This is the philosophic symbolist who is already emerging in the *Poems* of 1906 and who developed progressively in *The Listeners* (1912), *Motley* (1918), *The Viel* (1921) and *The Burning Glass* (1945). The two De la Mares overlap and the symbolist learnt much from the child poet as can be seen in some of the best poems in *The Listeners* like 'The Keys of the Morning':

> While at her bedroom window once,
> Learning her task for school,
> Little Louisa lonely sat
> In the morning clear and cool,
> She slanted her small bead-brown eyes
> Across the empty street,
> And saw Death softly watching her
> In the sunshine pale and sweet.
> His was a long lean sallow face
> He sat with half-shut eyes,
> Like an old sailor in a ship
> Becalmed 'neath tropic skies.

De la Mare used the world of childhood to provide symbols for his spiritual experience in much the same way as Yeats used Celtic mythology in his early poems. His weakness lies in his gift for subtle word music and his love of incantation. There is much truth in the criticism of I. A. Richards: 'His rhythm, that indescribable personal note, is a lulling rhythm, an anodyne, an opiate, it gives sleep and visions and phantasmagoria, but it does not give *vision*, it does not awaken'. In such poems as 'Arabia', that popular anthology piece, and the exquisite 'Music', De la Mare is providing an opiate for bored suburbans whose sensibility was too fine to be satisfied by Chesterton's noise and garish colour; in fact these poems bear the same relation to Chesterton's as Yeats's early poems to those of Kipling. In his later work De la Mare seems to be constantly striving to overcome the limitations of his dream-world of incantation and use his peculiar gifts to interpret the contemporary situation instead of to provide a refuge from it. He had not the advantage of living like Yeats in contact with a dynamic society full of political and artistic ferment like the Dublin of Synge and the Abbey Theatre. Sometimes he experimented in realistic poetry as in the powerful 'Drugged' and 'In the Dock' but his most interesting work is to be found when he comments on the contemporary situation from the view point of his own peculiar world as in 'Mrs Grundy', 'The Quiet Enemy' or the tragic vision of 'Awake':

> O self! O self! Wake from thy common sleep!
> Fling off the destroyer's net. He hath blinded and bound thee.
> In nakedness sit; pierce thy stagnation, and weep;
> Or corrupt in the grave—all Heaven around thee.

De la Mare lacks robustness and the heroic note, but he and

Chesterton showed that there was still a living and creative tradition of poetry in the middle-class England of the early twentieth century. There were other promising experiments too in the reign of Edward VII. Lascelles Abercrombie (1881–1938), was trained as a scientist at Manchester University, and later became a distinguished scholarly critic; he attempted a combination of philosophic dialogue and poetic drama in his *Interludes and Poems* of 1908, which he tried to develop on a grand scale in *Emblems of Love* of 1912. Like Matthew Arnold, Abercrombie was a remarkable poet whose genius was to a large extent stifled by academic theory. He believed that the long narrative poem on a grand scale could be revived and that the epic could assume new forms that would bring it back into repute as a living poetic form. *Emblems of Love* contains notable passages, but suffers from a kind of inflated sonorous loquacity and grandiose emptiness like that of Swinburne's later dramas. Abercrombie's best work is seen in some of his short poems like the admirable ironic 'Epitaph', and also in the use of his legend of St Thomas in a powerful one act play in verse, *The Sale of St Thomas* (1912), afterwards expanded into an epic drama in six acts with the same title (1931). Much of Abercrombie's work has a remoteness and an abstract quality which is no doubt due to the somewhat arid background of a teacher in the new universities of early twentieth-century England. In the legend of St Thomas, however, he found a subject that suited his powerful intellectual imagination. Gad's vision of the palace of souls in the expanded *Sale of St Thomas* has a rhythm which breaks through the bonds of the bardic tradition and is truly expressive of the modern 'schism in the soul', while the whole poem in spite of its legendary subject matter deals notably with the modern problem of the severance of the outer from the inner life and culminates in St Thomas's solution of the problem:

> He is the beauty he sees; and suddenly knows
> The two infinities that make the world—
> Infinite number of spirits in their life
> Of power on one another, and each spirit
> Infinite substance: the kingdom and the king!
> Then, feeling within himself one substance with all being,
> Again he looks within: and instantly
> Consumes in his own soul's unthinkable
> Immense of light; and for one heavenly moment,
> Himself the kingdom and himself the king,
> He is the glory of God and God in his glory.

This is rather a description in verse of a solution of the modern dilemma than an expression of a state of mind which has achieved such a solution. It is poetry which is about an attitude of mind conceived in the abstract rather than poetry arising out of an attitude of mind.

John Masefield (1878–1967) spent an adventurous youth at sea and for two years earned a living in America by doing odd jobs. Later he became a successful writer of poetry, plays and prose stories and ultimately succeeded Bridges as poet laureate in 1930. His *Salt Water Ballads* (1902) and *Ballads* (1903) combine a realism and vigour that recall some of the best of Kipling, together with a rather watery reflection of the romantic nostalgia of the early Yeats separated from its Irish background of living folk culture and adapted to the taste of English suburban readers. At times it seemed as though Masefield was going to be the heir of the Kipling of the 'Ballad of the Bolivar' as for instance in 'The Yarn of the Loch Achray':

> The dockside loafers talked on the quay
> The day that she towed down to sea:
> 'Lord what a handsome ship she be!
> Cheer her, sonny boys, three times three!'
> And the dockside loafers gave her a shout
> As the red-funnelled tug-boat towed her out. . . .

At other moments he seems to be the heir of the sentimentalised R.L.S. of the suburban bookshops and literary societies:

> O, the sea breeze will be steady, and the tall ship's going trim,
> And the dark blue skies are paling, and the white stars burning dim;
> And the long night watch is over, and the long sea-roving done,
> And yonder light is the Start Point light, and yonder comes the sun.

This is verse that suggests the 'arty crafty' teashop and the reproduction of the Academy picture rather than the life of the sailor. His best work is to be found in the narrative poems in which he revived Chaucerian metres with something of Chaucer's raciness and vividness (though none of his grace and wit) to tell stories of common English life with a strong emotional emphasis on the case for the underdog. 'The Everlasting Mercy' (1911), 'The Widow in the Bye Street' (1912), 'Dauber' (1913) and 'The Daffodil Fields' (1913) are the poetical counterparts of the emotional radicalism of Lloyd

George and the sentimental socialism of the young Ramsay Macdonald. They have the great merit of bringing poetry into touch
with the actualities of common life in contemporary England and
of putting into verse the language that Englishmen were actually
using in the pubs, the cottages and the streets. He never wrote
anything better than the scene in 'The Everlasting Mercy' in which
the drunken Saul Kane denounces his fellow townsmen:

> 'I am the fire. Back, stand back,
> Or else I'll fetch your skulls a crack;
> D'you see these copper nozzles here?
> They weigh ten pounds apiece, my dear;
> I'm fire of hell come up this minute
> To burn this town and all that's in it.
> To burn you dead and burn you clean,
> You cog-wheels in a stopped machine,
> You hearts of snakes, and brains of pigeons,
> You dead devout of dead religions. . . .'

Unfortunately the fire in Masefield went out when he went to
live near Bridges on Boar's Hill, and wrote stiff plays in verse and
vague spineless sonnets on Beauty. His old gift of racy realism,
however, reappears in the fine impressionist sketches of English
country life in 'Reynard the Fox' (1919) and 'Right Royal' (1920).
It is, perhaps, not without significance that Ramsay Macdonald's
government recommended Masefield's appointment to the
laureateship. He was a kind of Ramsay Macdonald of poetry,
starting his career as a fiery revolutionary and ending it as a champ-
ion of gentlemanly decorum.

William Henry Davies (1871-1940), like Masefield, enjoyed the
advantages of avoiding a conventional education and of seeing life
from the angle of the poor man. Unlike Masefield, however, he
was not attracted by suburban refinement, but was a born tramp
who loved the freedom of the outcast and voluntarily spent years
on the roads and in the doss-houses of England and America.
Born in a public house in Newport, he was brought up by Non-
conformist grandparents and apprenticed to a picture frame maker.
The death of his grandmother left him with a tiny income, and
obtaining fifteen pounds from her trustee he embarked for America
where he lived the life of a tramp for five years. Finally he returned
to England where he began to write poetry, and hawked a few
of his poems from door to door in order to raise enough money to

publish a volume. This volume, *The Soul's Destroyer*, was published in 1902 but failed to attract any notice till he sent it to Bernard Shaw, who at once recognised the quality of Davies's genius. 'His work', Shaw wrote, 'was not in the least strenuous or modern: there was in it no sign that he had read anything later than Cowper or Crabbe . . . there was indeed no sign of his having read anything otherwise than as a child reads. The result was a freedom from literary vulgarity which was like a draught of clear water in a desert. Here, I saw, was a genuine innocent writing odds and ends of verse about odds and ends of things.' Davies was in fact a modern 'primitive', a sort of 'Sunday painter' or Douanier Rousseau of English poetry who had been preserved from the blight of twentieth-century standardised pseudo-culture by living among the 'prisoners' of the capitalist world. His pellucid little nature lyrics have often been praised and anthologised, but his most interesting and characteristic work is to be found in his vivid sketches of the Edwardian underworld:

> There's 'Scotty' Bill, four score of years,
>   Who every morning when we rise,
> Will swear that summer's not yet come,
>   And question us—'Where are the flies?'
> .   .   .   .
> I asked a lodger—'tell me why
>   Bill swears, and where his trouble lies.'
> 'Old Bill makes sticky papers, and
>   He makes his living catching flies.'
> .   .   .   .
> And Bill, he knows a thing or two,
>   For here he sticks the cursed cause
> That robbed sweet summer of her flies—
>   ''Tis those damn sanitation laws.'

This is not ambitious poetry, but it arises out of a way of life as surely as the medieval ballads or the courtly lyrics of the seventeenth century. Davies is the last heir of the old English proletarian tradition of Elderton, Deloney, Henry Carey and the broadside poets.

After the death of the old king, the political crisis of 1910–11 and the Agadir incident, the whole structure of English society was subjected to a tension which foreshadowed the coming storm. This was the period of the birth of 'Georgian poetry': the Georgian 'movement' in itself was neither a revolution nor a revival. Rather it represents a phase of that revival of English poetry which had accompanied the resurgence of Liberal England in the reign of Edward VII. Indeed it might well be described as a gradual petering out of that revival parallel to the dying of the liberal spirit in politics which began about 1911 and extended to 1919. *Georgian Poetry* was the title given to a series of anthologies edited by Edward Marsh (1872–1953) (afterwards Sir Edward Marsh), a civil servant with a talent for friendship with poets and a gift for verse-translation. Sir Edward's first volume of *Georgian Poetry* appeared in 1912. It included contributions by a number of writers who had made their reputations in the reign of Edward VII such as Chesterton, De la Mare, Abercrombie and W. H. Davies. The most memorable poetry in it is indeed to be found in the one act version of Abercrombie's *Sale of St Thomas* with which it opens, and some lyrics from De la Mare's *The Listeners*. Taken as a whole, however, it is a strange collection to represent English poetry at the moment when Europe was preparing for the First World War and England's stability was being rocked by the constitutional crisis and the impending disruption of the Protestant Ascendancy in Ireland. The smooth rhythms and pleasant homely landscapes of most of the poems in it belong to the England of 'the rich man in his castle, the poor man at his gate', which Masterman noted as an anachronism in 1908. The essential England of 1912, the England of the great cities is only glimpsed in two short poems, one by W. W. Gibson and one by W. H. Davies. The England of the machines and the factories and the England of the suburbs are wholly absent. It is a very insular collection. Nobody would guess from it that Blériot had recently made the first flight in an aeroplane across the Channel or that there had been an abortive Russian revolution or that Germany was preparing to dominate Europe. There is, of course, no need for poets to comment directly or indirectly on contemporary politics or social life (though most of the great ones have done so), but poetry which grows out of a fully developed and integrated sensibility necessarily reflects in its rhythms and imagery the quality of contemporary life, as those of Marlowe's plays reflect the violence and splendour of the age of Elizabeth and Drake and those of Pope's satires the irony and sceptical grace of the age of Bolingbroke and Voltaire. 'I liked poetry', wrote Sir Edward Marsh, 'to be all three (or if not all three, at least two; or if the worst came to the worst at least one) of the following things: intelligible, musical and racy, and I was happier with it if it was written on some formal principle which I could

discern, and from which it departed, if at all, only for the sake of
some special effect, and not because the lazy or too impetuous
writer had found observance difficult or irksome. I liked poetry
that I wanted to know by heart, and *could* learn by heart if I had
time.'[1] Poetry is conceived here as the product of a craftsman who
should work on traditional lines. It is to be an artefact providing a
pastime for the leisure of a governing class. Innovation is discouraged because it interfered with the ease with which the connoisseur
could obtain pleasant sensations from the volume which he had
purchased. Such a critical attitude might produce minor poetry of
merit; it could hardly be conducive to the writing of the poetry
which is a spiritual adventure and a fresh exploration of reality.
The tradition on which Sir Edward Marsh and his friends had been
brought up was that of the great English nature poets of the early
nineteenth century. *Georgian Poetry* is thus full of imitations of
Romantic nature poetry which bear much the same relation to
the poetry of Wordsworth and Keats as that which the landscapes of
contemporary academicians bore to those of Turner and Constable.
Every one of the Georgian anthologies contains many lines like
the following by John Drinkwater:

> I turned me from the place in humble wise,
> And fingers soft were laid upon mine eyes,
> And I beheld the fruitful earth, with store
> Of odorous treasure, full and golden grain,
> Ripe orchard bounty, slender stalks that bore
> Their flowered beauty with a meek content.

This is Keats and water, or to apply the cruel phrase of F. R. Leavis,
'The vulgarity of Keats with a public school accent'. These words
were actually used with reference to the work of Rupert Brooke
(1887–1915), the handsome and brilliant son of a Rugby house-
master, who enchanted his contemporaries at Cambridge and was
elected to a Fellowship at King's. Brooke was the star performer
in the original Georgian troupe and he is said to have suggested
the plan of the collection to Marsh. He was a wonderfully accom-
plished versifier in the manner that was orthodox among the
pundits of public school culture in his day, but his mind remained
to the end that of a clever public schoolboy. Among the poems
which he contributed to the first volume of *Georgian Poetry* is the

---

[1] *A Number of People* (1939), p. 322.

well known 'Grantchester', which can be fairly taken as the type
of the Georgian poem:

> Ah God! to see the branches stir
> Across the moon at Grantchester!
> To smell the thrilling-sweet and rotten
> Unforgettable, unforgotten
> River smell, and hear the breeze
> Sobbing in the little trees.
> Say, do the elm-clumps greatly stand
> Still guardians of that holy land?
> The chestnuts shade, in reverend dream,
> The yet unacademic stream?
> Is dawn a secret shy and cold
> Anadyomene, silver-gold?
> And sunset still a golden sea
> From Haslingfield to Madingley?
> And after, ere the night is born,
> Do hares come out about the corn?
> Oh, is the water sweet and cool,
> Gentle and brown, above the pool?
> And laughs the immortal river still
> Under the mill, under the mill?
> Say, is there Beauty yet to find
> And Certainty? And Quiet kind?
> Deep meadows yet, for to forget
> The lies, the truths, and pain? ... Oh! yet
> Stands the Church clock at ten to three?
> And is there honey still for tea?

This is a pastoralism which is not, like the pastoralism of the
Elizabethans, the creation of a vivid, ideal way of living, the
heightening of elements in contemporary life. Rather it is a poetry
that deliberately turns away from the contemporary situation (the
lies, the truths, and pain) and uses the daydream of an unspoiled
English countryside as an anodyne. It is the fantasy of an upper
middle class which feared reality and refused to face the modern
crisis at the very moment when it was assuming dimensions that
threatened to disrupt the whole of the European social structure.
Brooke was too intelligent to shut his eyes completely to the
ugliness of the modern world. He even tried to make poetry out
of it, and he seems to have invented[1] the trick of producing a

---

[1] Or perhaps he caught it from Hilaire Belloc (1870-1953) who used it with
excellent effect in his brilliant epigrams.

humorous effect by using the sonorous rhythms of classic English poetry ironically to deal with ugly or absurd subject matter:

> Opposite me two Germans snore and sweat.
>   Through sullen swirling gloom we jolt and roar.
> We have been here for ever: even yet
>   A dim watch tells two hours, two aeons, more.
> The windows are tight-shut and slimy wet. . . .

There is promise of a better poet here than the day-dreamer of 'Grantchester', but even snoring, sweating Germans are viewed from the angle of a superior British upper middle class, which finds in them the sort of whimsical humour that it might find in a monkey at the Zoo.

Five volumes of Georgian poetry were published, the last appearing as late at 1922. These volumes included work by such writers as D. H. Lawrence and Robert Graves who really had no connection with the Georgian fold. The best work of the typical Georgians such as J. C. Squire, John Freeman, Edward Shanks and Francis Brett Young is an unambitious, limited pictorial sort of poetry comparable with that of some of Johnson's minor eighteenth-century poets like Pomfret, though it lacks the sense of a contact with a living social background which is the strength of even the minor Augustans. Much other verse of the Georgians, however, justifies the name of 'week-end poets', which was applied to them in the nineteen-twenties, and the satire on their 'hostel' furnished in 'Ye Olde Teashoppe Style' in Roy Campbell's *The Georgiad* (1931).

Two poets of this period succeeded in creating a more genuine and satisfying pastoralism than the 'over-vegetated'[1] fantasies of the Drinkwaters and the Freemans. For both, the English country-side was a living reality and not merely a pleasant view from the window of a week-end cottage. The elder of the two was Edward Thomas (1878–1917), who made a reputation as a writer of prose essays, stories and critical studies, and only began to write verse at the age of thirty at the suggestion of his friend, Robert Frost, the American poet. Two small volumes of his verse appeared after he was killed in action in France in 1917. None of Thomas's poems appeared in *Georgian Poetry*, but many of them achieve the effects that the best of the Georgians seem to have aimed at, while they

---

[1] I owe the adjective to a review of *Georgian Poetry 1918–1919* by Siegfried Sassoon published in *The New York Times* of February, 1920.

are remarkably free from the literary vulgarity of a bookish clique
which disfigures too much Georgian poetry. The sights and sounds
of the English countryside are not anodynes for this poet, but, as
Aldous Huxley has pointed out in his excellent essay on him, they
awaken in him 'nameless and indescribable emotions' which he
expresses with a Wordsworthian honesty:

> It seems I have no tears left. They should have fallen—
> Their ghosts, if tears have ghosts, did fall—that day
> When twenty hounds streamed by me, not yet combed out
> But still all equals in their rage of gladness
> Upon the scent, made one, like a great dragon
> In Blooming Meadow that bends towards the sun
> And once bore hops. . . .

The rhythm of these lines is no mere mechanical tune, but is
inflected in such a way that it expresses the animal energy of the
hounds, the brilliance of the meadow and the poet's shock of joyful
surprise, which is rendered magnificently by the image of the
dragon.

Edmund Blunden (1896–   ), one of the youngest contributors
to *Georgian Poetry*, is a meditative and elegiac poet who resembles
Thomas in his quiet integrity and his close observation of the
English country scene. He revived with much success the old
English tradition of the unassuming realistic poetry of rural life,
the tradition of Cowper, Crabbe and Clare:

> When on the green the rag-tag game had stopt
> And red the lights through alehouse curtains glowed.
> The clambering brake drove out and took the road.
> Then on the stern moors all the babble dropt
> Among our merry men, who felt the dew
> Sweet to the soul and saw the southern blue
> Thronged with heat lightning miles and miles abroad,
> Working and whickering, snakish, winged and clawed,
> Or like old carp lazily rising and shouldering.
> Long the slate cloud flame shook with the death-white smouldering:
> Yet not a voice. . . .

This is not the country as seen by a tourist with a sentimental
attachment to an imaginary unspoilt England. It is the spirit of the
English countryside expressed by one who has lived close to it
and knows its people, their speech and way of thinking. In his later

work Blunden has achieved an unpretentious yet dignified humanity which suggests that he should be considered rather as the heir of Thomas Hardy than as a belated Georgian.

6

TRENCH POETS, IMAGISTS AND
D. H. LAWRENCE

I. TRENCH POETS

In August, 1914, the modern crisis passed into a new phase which has lasted to our own time. In this phase the forces which had been latent for over a quarter of a century behind the apparently stable facade of 'capitalist' society became active and began visibly to destroy or transform the structure which had stood firm since the Renaissance. The actual outbreak of war was greeted with a surge of enthusiasm which transcended all bounds of class and party and was unlike anything in previous English history. Earlier English wars (with the partial exception of the Civil War of the seventeenth century) had been mainly affairs of the governing class. Whatever the motives of members of that class may have been in 1914, the war was, at the outset at any rate, an affair of the whole nation, passionately convinced that it was embarking on a crusade for a righteous cause. To find a parallel to the spirit of hundreds of thousands of young men who gave up comfortable homes and civilian jobs to join the New Armies it would be necessary to go back to the armies of Revolutionary France in 1792 or, on a smaller scale, to the Independents of Cromwell's New Model Army of 1644. Part of the enthusiasm was certainly due to the sense of relief from the intolerable tension of the years immediately preceding the war and from the drabness and monotony of commercialised 'civilisation', part probably to a sense of the breaking down of the barriers of British insularity and a reassertion of unity with the rest of Europe and the outer world. Part of it also was the outcome of the moral sense derived from the English puritan tradition, which had been starved, corrupted, but not killed in a world of competitive commerce, and which now seemed to have found an outlet in heroic action. Many attempts were made by poets to express the enthusiasm of the first months of the war. The problem was to create a myth which would give poetic form to the inner meaning of the crisis. Most of these attempts failed because the poets did not understand that this was not a war of the old type and could only think of it in terms of conventional patriotism. They had not learned the lessen tersely summarised in Edith Cavell's famous saying: 'Patriotism is not enough'. The one adequate poetic expression of the spirit of young Englishmen in 1914 was the 'Song of the Soldiers' of the septuagenarian Thomas Hardy dated September, 1914:

> What of the faith and fire within us
>   Men who march away
>   Ere the barn-cocks say
>   Dawn is growing gray,
> Leaving all that here can win us;
> What of the faith and fire within us
>   Men who march away?

The rhythm of this poem is the rhythm of marching men; it is a rhythm also that expresses the reawakening of the adventurous spirit that had been stifled for so long by the dullness of urbanised industrialism. Hardy, too, has found words for the supremely significant fact that, for the first time since 1642, a British Army was fighting for a moral cause and a cause which it understood. Hardy's citizen soldiers, who 'well know what they are doing', can be contrasted with Tennyson's professional Victorian troopers:

> Theirs not to reason why,
> Theirs but to do and die.

Rupert Brooke joined the newly formed Naval Division, was present at the unsuccessful attempt to relieve Antwerp, and died in the Aegean on his way to Gallipoli in 1915. His celebrated sonnet sequence, '1914', expresses in glossy melodious conventional verse of the bardic type the attitudes towards the war which were common among Englishmen in the autumn of 1914. The first was the sense of release from the dullness of an ignoble industrialised world, the second the emotional patriotism which regarded the war as a defence of a beautiful English against a brutal enemy and the third an idealisation of those who gave their lives in the struggle.

All these attitudes were perfectly natural at the beginning of the war, but they were soon cheapened and exploited by politicians and journalists. In Brooke's sonnets they are exploited, not deliberately, but in a naive way by a writer whose sensibility was always that of a clever, attractive schoolboy. They are poems which are managed by mass emotions as opposed to poems like Hardy's on the South African War or Yeats's on the Irish Rebellion, where the poetry controls the emotion. It is instructive to compare the most celebrated of the sonnets (no. V, 'The Soldier') with Hardy's 'Drummer Hodge' (see p. 41):

> If I should die, think only this of me:
>   That there's some corner of a foreign field
> That is for ever England. There shall be
>   In that rich earth a richer dust concealed. . . .

Hardy accepts the brutal fact that Hodge's 'homely Northern breast and brain' will be turned into 'some Southern tree' on the Karoo and the effect of his poem arises from his power of conveying the terror and mystery of that change as well as the intense pathos of the death of the boy in a remote country of which he was profoundly ignorant. Brooke, allowing his emotion to master his poetry, presents the reader with a boyish fantasy which pretends that the earth where the dead soldier lies will become 'England' and that his dust is 'richer' than the earth of the surrounding country. All the images and rhythms of the 1914 sonnets are smooth and pleasant, but they ring hollow and they belong to a world of beautiful fictions which turned away from the terrible reality of modern warfare.

   Another form of the idealisation of the war in the early phase is found in the single well-known poem of the Honourable Julian Grenfell, one of the brilliant sons of Lord Desborough. For Grenfell the polo-player, pig-sticker and professional cavalry officer, the war was a major sporting event. His poetry was as much of an anachronism in 1915 as the cavalry to which he belonged, but the rhythms and images of his 'Into Battle' have less literary vulgarity than those of Brooke's sonnets, and really express in an amateurish way some part of the physical grace and energy of those favoured young English aristocrats who grew to manhood in the 'sweet and carefree' atmosphere of the English upper class world of 1913–14 so admirably described by Sir Osbert Sitwell in *Great Morning:*

> The fighting man shall from the sun
>   Take warmth, and life from the glowing earth;
> Speed with the light-foot wind to run,
>   And with the trees to newer birth;
> And find, when fighting shall be done,
>   Great rest, and fullness after dearth.

A large quantity of verse was written by young poets in the early months of the war. 'Scores of slim volumes and hundreds of separate poems have come from men in the army—from France and Flanders, Gallipoli and the Soudan, Egypt and East Africa', writes the editor of an anthology of *Soldier Poets* which appeared in 1916. Most of this verse is of poor quality and reveals the pitiful inadequacy of the debased tradition of English middle-class culture to deal with the crisis in European civilisation.

The credit of being the first English poet of the war generation to explore the profounder meaning of the crisis and to express some measure of its true significance belongs to Charles Hamilton Sorley (1895–1915), the son of a Cambridge professor of philosophy. Sorley, who was killed on the Western Front on 13 October, 1915, had written some remarkable verse while he was still at school at Marlborough. Like most of his contemporaries, he overestimated the importance of Masefield's early narratives, but he clearly perceives the hollowness of the literary English poetry of his time. 'The voice of our poets and men of letters is finely trained and sweet to hear; it teems with sharp saws and rich sentiment: it is a marvel of delicate technique: it pleases, it flatters, it charms, it soothes: it is a living lie.' Dr I. A. Richards remarked that Rupert Brooke's poetry had no inside; Sorley had made the 'voyage within' and his poems have a solidity that contrasts with the hollowness of the smooth verses of the Georgians. These poems embody attitudes to the war which are quite different from those of Brooke and Grenfell. One of these attitudes is a sense of aimlessness and frustration, of being part of a huge machine that functions in an inhuman and incomprehensible way. This is already apparent in a poem written as early as September 1914:

> A hundred thousand million mites we go
> Wheeling and tacking o'er the eternal plain,
> Some black with death—some are white with woe.
> Who sent us forth? Who takes us home again?

Then there is a much more mature attitude to the international crisis. Sorley had lived in Germany and had a deep understanding and appreciation of German literature and the German spirit. His sonnet addressed to Germany shows the war not as a defence of an ideally beautiful England against a wicked enemy but as a tragic cleavage between two great nations blinded by hatred:

> You are blind like us. Your hurt no man designed,
> And no man claimed the conquest of your land.
> But gropers both through fields of thought confined
> We stumble and we do not understand.
> You only saw your future bigly planned,
> And we the tapering paths of our own mind,
> And in each other's dearest ways we stand,
> And hiss and hate. And the blind fight the blind.

The author of these lines has not only learnt with his intellect that 'patriotism is not enough'; he has transmuted the thought into poetry.

There is also a new attitude to the fallen. Death in action is no longer regarded as beautiful and heroic, but as terrible and piteous, too terrible for cheap emotion. Sorley's sonnet to the dead, probably the last poem that he wrote[1], is the first competent attempt to deal with this difficult theme; it anticipates the spirit and the methods of Wilfred Owen:

> When you see millions of the mouthless dead
> Across your dreams in pale battalions go,
> Say not soft things as other men have said,
> That you'll remember. For you need not so.
> Give them not praise. For, deaf, how should they know
> It is not curses heaped on each gashed head?
> Nor tears. Their blind eyes see not your tears flow.
> Nor honour. It is easy to be dead.

By 1916 a great change in English society had taken place, a change which was the beginning of the end of the old social system. Cutting across the old horizontal class divisions and tending to obliterate them, was a new vertical division between the nation at home, which, except for a few air raids, had not suffered at all from the war, and indeed had to a considerable extent benefited by it, and the nation overseas, the new community of the vast armies on

---

[1] According to the Preface to the third edition of *Marlborough and Other Poems* this poem was 'found in his kit sent back from France'.

the Continent, living in the filth and discomfort of the trenches under continuous shell fire and subjected to gas attacks, trench mortar bombardments and the other amenities of mechanised warfare. There was a growing cleavage between these two nations. The nation at home still believed in the patriotic myth of a beautiful, heroic war against diabolic enemies. The nation overseas was in touch with realities of life and death, and was completely disillusioned with regard to the heroic nature of the struggle. Indeed as the war went on, they became more and more solidly united in sentiment not against the Germans, but against (as it appeared to them) the callous, stupid nation at home, the government and, above all, the 'brass-hats' of the staff. More and more as the new armies grew, the nation overseas came to resemble not the old army with its reproduction of the civilian social structure, but a classless (though not a democratic) society governed by an *élite* of officers promoted from the ranks. This new community produced a few remarkable writers, who made poetry out of the moral revulsion against war which was the mood of the finest spirits of the nation overseas in the period 1916–1918. These poets were the true heirs of the revival of liberal middle-class culture which had begun about 1905, and, as far as poetry was concerned, had petered out in the amiable dilettantism of the Georgians. In the tense atmosphere of the nation overseas it blazed up fiercely for the last time in an outburst of indignation and pity which was far truer to the spirit of the 'men who marched away' in 1914 than the emotional patriotism of the journalists and the politicians.

Siegfried Sassoon (1886–1967) was the pioneer of the new kind of war poetry. In 1914 he was a young man with a comfortable private income, whose interests were hunting and poetry; he had written several volumes of verse, which had been privately printed, and he had been encouraged by Sir Edmund Gosse. His most remarkable literary achievement before the war, however, had been a brilliant parody of Masefield's 'The Everlasting Mercy' called 'The Daffodil Murderer' which had appeared under the pseudonym of Saul Kane in 1913.[1] 'The Daffodil Murderer' is not only a remarkably clever imitation of Masefield's style, but a moving and original poem, superior in some ways to Masefield's. It is significant, too, because it shows that even before the war Sassoon had a sense of the hollowness of the gentlemanly paradise in which he spent his youth, and a deep sympathy for the common man who

[1] Regrettably Sassoon has not reprinted this poem in his *Collected Poems*. But see the appendix to *Siegfried Sassoon a Critical Study*, by Michael Thorpe (1966).

was excluded from that paradise. The poems that he wrote in the
early years of the war are in the Georgian manner; he was admitted
to the circle of Sir Edward Marsh and on the single occasion on
which he met Rupert Brooke he regarded him with awe as 'a
being singled out for some transplendent performance, some
enshrined achievement'.[1] In his early war poems he could still
echo Brooke's greeting to war as a heroic deliverance:

> For we have made an end of all things base;
> We are returning by the road we came:

He was, however, too honest and too sensitive to continue to live
in this world of romantic fantasy, and by 1916 he was writing
verses filled with intense sympathy for the sufferings of his fellow-
soldiers, and indignation at the stupid cruelty of war:

> And then he thought: to-morrow night we trudge
> Up to the trenches, and my boots are rotten.
> Five miles of stodgy clay and freezing sludge,
> And everything but wretchedness forgotten.
> To-night he's in the pink; but soon he'll die.
> And still the war goes on; *he* don't know why.

Sassoon was at his best when he combined this pity for the ordeal of
the common soldier with a savage irony directed against the stupidity
and vulgarity of the people who shut their eyes to the horror of the
war. In a few burning verses, which have a satiric 'bite' unequalled
since Byron, he became the voice of the contempt of the nation
overseas for the callousness and imbecility that disgusted thousands
of soldiers who returned from shell-torn, rat-infested trenches to
the amusements which were supposed to cheer the war-worn
heroes:

> The House is crammed: tier beyond tier they grin
> And cackle at the Show, while prancing ranks
> Of harlots shrill the chorus, drunk with din;
> 'We're sure the Kaiser loves the dear old Tanks!'
>
> I'd like to see a Tank come down the stalls,
> Lurching to rag-time tunes, or 'Home, Sweet Home,'—
> And there'd be no more jokes in Music-Halls
> To mock the riddled corpses round Bapaume.

---

[1] *The Weald of Youth*, p. 231.

E

Sassoon had no originality in technique. He used the smooth rhymed decasyllabics of the Georgians in nearly all the poems and he seems to have learnt from Brooke's realistic poems (see p. 118) the trick of producing a humorous effect by the contrast between a stately traditional metre and subject matter very unlike the dignified themes with which such metres are associated. There is nearly always a touch of parody in Sassoon's war poems and sometimes it is used with devastating effect as in the lines called 'Base Details' which echo Yeats's 'When you are old' (see p. 80):

> If I were fierce, and bald, and short of breath,
>   I'd live with scarlet Majors at the Base,
> And speed glum heroes up the line to death.
>   You'd see me with my puffy petulant face,
> Guzzling and gulping in the best hotel,
>   Reading the Roll of Honour. . . .

Sassoon's best poetry is to be found in these powerful little satires. It lives by its passionate sincerity and honesty, but it is purely destructive. It performed the great service of debunking the old romantic myth of the glory of the war, but it created no new myth to express the inner meaning of the conflict and the crisis of which it was a symptom. Its form and its sentiment are unrelated except by the contrast of parody, and this was a device which had no promise for the future.

Sassoon's poetry, however, is notable for other reasons besides its intrinsic merit. Its immediate influence was considerable and it stimulated the development of the most remarkable of all the English poets of the First World War, Wilfred Owen (1893–1918). Owen came from an obscure provincial middle-class family. Thus he had the good fortune to avoid a public school education, and he was also lucky in getting into touch with French culture at an early age. He was educated at a school at Birkenhead, spent a short time at University College, Reading, and after a serious illness went to Bordeaux as a tutor in a French family in 1913. There he made the acquaintance of one of the most interesting French poets of the time, the veteran symbolist Laurent Tailhade, a daring experimenter in poetic technique and subject matter, and an original and powerful thinker with strong pacifist views for which he had suffered imprisonment. Owen returned to England in 1915, when he enlisted in the Artists' Rifles. He received a commission in the Manchester Regiment and went to the Somme battlefield in the terrible winter of 1916–17. He was invalided home in June, 1917, and sent to Craiglockhart hospital near Edinburgh, where, by a lucky chance, Sassoon also came in August to be treated for 'shell shock' as a result of his public protest against the war. Sassoon's friendship and encouragement were of incalculable value to the younger poet. Owen returned to France at the end of August 1918. On November 4th, a week before the Armistice, he was killed in the fighting on the Sambre Canal.

Owen wrote clever verses, strongly influenced by Keats, when he was still a boy. The surviving specimens have a lush sensuousness like that of the early Hopkins. There can be little doubt that the powerful originality of Tailhade and the formal experiments of contemporary French poetry influenced him considerably. They probably saved him from the imitation of the weaker aspects of English romantic poetry which is so apparent in the work of the Georgians. His earliest poem on the war, a sonnet called 'The Seed', in spite of its immaturity, has a prophetic power which is very unlike the polished hollowness of Rupert Brooke's '1914':

> War broke. And now the winter of the world
> With perishing great darkness closes in.
> The cyclone of the pressure on Berlin
> Is over all the width of Europe whirled.

Already in 1914, this nineteen-year-old poet had seen the war not as a heroic deliverance but as a terrible international disaster, 'the winter of the world'. The first of his great poems on the suffering of the war, 'Exposure', written early in 1917, is already not an ironic or compassionate statement or description like Sassoon's war poems, but an unforgettable re-creation in poetic form of the misery and boredom of the infantryman in the trenches:

> Our brains ache, in the merciless iced east winds that knive us. . . .
> Wearied we keep awake because the night is silent. . . .
> Low, drooping flares confuse our memories of the salient. . . .
> Worried by silence, sentries whisper, curious, nervous,
> But nothing happens.
>
> Watching we hear the mad gusts tugging on the wire,
> Like twitching agonies of men among its brambles.
> Northward, incessantly, the flickering gunnery rumbles,
> Far off, like a dull rumour of some other war.
> What are we doing here?

Owen is not a satirist or a parodist like Sassoon; he is a prophet and a myth-maker. In the famous fragment of a Preface to the projected volume of poems which he left unpublished at his death, he wrote:

> Above all I am not concerned with Poetry.
> My subject is War, and the pity of War.
> The Poetry is in the pity.

The word 'poetry' in the first of these sentences seems to mean 'poetry' in the conventional, romantic sense of the word. His 'poetry' was not to be found in beauty of rhythms or images. It was 'in the pity'. He did not write *about* his pity. His poetry *was* his pity. The best illustration of this profound statement is to be found in the poem called 'Greater Love' in which, with a passionate wit recalling that of Donne or Marvell, he sets beside the gentle, sexual images which are the stuff of 'poetry' in the romantic sense, the terrible and violent images of war with their far more powerful 'poetry' which is 'in the pity'.

> Red lips are not so red
>   As the stained stones kissed by the English dead.
> Kindness of wooed and wooer
> Seems shame to their love pure.
> O Love, your eyes lose lure
>   When I behold eyes blinded in my stead!
>
> Your slender attitude
>   Trembles not exquisite like limbs knife-skewed,
> Rolling and rolling there
> Where God seems not to care;
> Till the fierce Love they bear
>   Cramps them in death's extreme decrepitude.

Owen has the power, already hinted at in the last poems of Sorley, to whom he is really closer in many ways than to Sassoon, of seeing the landscape of war in terms of apocalyptic vision:

> My soul looked down from a vague height with Death,
> As unremembering how I rose or why,
> And saw a sad land, weak with sweats of dearth,
> Gray, cratered like the moon with hollow woe,
> And pitted with great pocks and scabs of plagues.
>
> Across its beard, that horror of harsh wire,
> There moved thin caterpillars, slowly uncoiled.

> It seemed they pushed themselves to be as plugs
> Of ditches, where they writhed and shrivelled, killed.

The famous little elegy 'Futility' has a cosmic grandeur in its image of the sun's age-old influence on the earth, and a truly tragic irony in the contrast of the 'kind old sun' and the 'fatuous sunbeams' with human cruelty:

> Think how it wakes the seeds,—
> Woke, once, the clays of a cold star.
> Are limbs, so dear achieved, are sides,
> Full-nerved—still warm—too hard to stir?
> Was it for this that clay grew tall?
> —O what made fatuous sunbeams toil
> To break earth's sleep at all?

Owen's greatest achievement is the fragment called 'Strange Meeting', which has a solemn magnificence, recalling Keats's revised version of 'Hyperion'. Here his favourite device of 'para-rhyme' (consonant rhyme with vowel dissonance) creates a remarkable effect (to quote the words of Edmund Blunden) of 'remoteness, darkness, emptiness, shock, echo'. In this poem, 'patriotism is not enough', which Sorley had translated into a truly poetic statement in his sonnet 'To Germany', is re-created as a great prophetic myth. In a 'profound dull tunnel' like those of the Hindenburg Line, the poet comes on 'encumbered sleepers', one of whom springs up, and stares with piteous recognition in fixed eyes. He is both the enemy who has been killed and the poet himself, humanity transcending the cleavage of War:

> 'Strange friend,' I said, 'here is no cause to mourn.'
> 'None,' said the other, 'save the undone years,
> The hopelessness. Whatever hope is yours,
> Was my life also; I went hunting wild
> After the wildest beauty in the world. . . .
> . . . .
> Now men will go content with what we spoiled.
> Or, discontent, boil bloody, and be spilled.
> They will be swift with swiftness of the tigress,
> None will break ranks, though nations trek from progress.
> Courage was mine, and I had mystery;
> Wisdom was mine, and I had mastery;
> To miss the march of this retreating world
> Into vain citadels that are not walled.'

In this prophetic passage Owen seems to foretell the possibility of a world split into rival ideologies of left and right, where the free spirit could no longer live:

'None will break ranks, though nations trek from progress' is a remarkable prophecy of the fascist and communist totalitarian states the direct outcome of the war, which Owen, far more clearly than any of his contemporaries, saw as a poisoning of the whole European tradition.

The greatness of Owen's poetry lies in its moral power. It is based on a morality that is the result of a profound exploration of the inner life, which, strangely enough, in the misery of trench-warfare has here found for an instant a more complete synthesis with outward experience than in any English poet since Hopkins. Owen had a profoundly religious mind. He was unable to retain his belief in orthodox Christianity, but the pacifism of Tailhade gave him a kind of 'religion of humanity', and the indignation and pity arising out of his war experience had the quality of a 'conversion'. Like the Jesuit training of Hopkins, it purifies his inner life and gave him a new vision of the outer world, not a joyous vision of nature like that of Hopkins in peaceful Victorian England, but a terrible one which was nevertheless made divine by the quality of common humanity:

> I, too, saw God through mud,—
> The mud that cracked on cheeks when wretches smiled.
> War brought more glory to their eyes than blood,
> And gave their laughs more glee than shakes a child.

Owen had not the scholarly equipment of Hopkins, but like Hopkins, he was a great renovator of English poetic form. In certain poems he succeeds in creating a new idiom and new sound patterns which express typically modern states of mind and yet also bear a definite relation to traditional forms:

> But cursed are dullards whom no cannon stuns,
> That they should be as stones;
> Wretched are they, and mean
> With paucity that never was simplicity.
> By choice they made themselves immune
> To pity and whatever moans in man
> Before the last sea and the hapless stars;
> Whatever moans when many leave these shores;
> Whatever shares
> The eternal reciprocity of tears.

In such a passage as this not only the skilful use of para-rhyme but the very structure of the sentences and movement of the verse express the 'schism in the soul'. Intense emotion is not only felt but controlled and turned into significant form.

Alone among the other Trench Poets of 1917–18 Isaac Rosenberg (1880–1918), a young Jewish painter, who served as a private in the infantry and was killed in the retreat from the Somme in April 1918, had an apocalyptic vision of the horror of modern warfare comparable with that of Owen:

> The plunging limbers over the shattered track
> Racketed with their rusty freight,
> Stuck out like many crowns of thorns,
> And the rusty stakes like sceptres old
> To stay the flood of brutish men
> Upon our brothers dear.
>
> The wheels lurched over sprawled dead
> But pained them not, though their bones crunched,
> Their shut mouths made no moan.
> They lie there huddled, friend and foeman,
> Man born of man, and born of woman,
> And shells go crying over them
> From night till night and now.

This remarkable poet has been most unjustly neglected, and it is time that justice was done to his brilliant though fragmentary achievement.

In his memoir, *Siegfried's Journey*, Sassoon writes of his ambition in 1918 to 'do something on a bigger scale' and describe the war 'in a comprehensive way, seeing it like a painter'. This ambition was never fulfilled, but something like it was achieved by David Jones (1895–   ), an Anglo-Welsh engraver, painter and student of early Welsh literature, who served as a private in Sassoon's regiment, and published in 1937 *In Parenthesis*, which may be described as the one English poem of epic dimensions and quality which came out of the First World War. Jones had several advantages over the Trench Poets. When he wrote, a sufficiently long time had elapsed since the end of the war to enable him to 'distance' his experiences in a way which was impossible for those who were actually involved in the fighting. His knowledge of early literature enabled him to link himself to a heroic tradition which was not vulgarised like the 'heroic' attitudes which Sassoon and Owen rejected. Finally, he was able to profit by the stylistic experiments of

Joyce, Eliot and Pound, whose works he had obviously studied carefully. His poem (the word is used advisedly, although *In Parenthesis* is written in a mixture of prose and free verse), like Eliot's *Waste Land* and Joyce's *Ulysses*, is characterised by an interpenetration of the present with the past. It represents the experience of John Ball, a private of 'Kitchener's Army', who goes with his battalion to France and into action on the Somme, where many of his comrades are killed and he himself is wounded. Jones does not use conventional narrative but conveys the action by a series of scenes and images, with frequent juxtaposition of quotations and allusions to early literature and legend, by means of which Ball's experience is connected with that of earlier soldiers notably those of Shakespeare's *Henry V* and of *Y Goddodin*, a sixth century Welsh epic lay commemorating a desperate foray of Celtic tribesmen in the North of England. Jones's quotations and allusions are not used with ironic intent like those in Eliot's *The Waste Land*, but rather, as Bergonzi has pointed out, to transfigure 'by the light of earlier heroes' 'the humble infantryman enduring the misery of the trenches'. This powerful and highly original work does not lend itself easily to quotation but the following portrayal of the deaths of a Welsh and a Jewish soldier is a typical example of Jones's richly allusive style, his compassionate but unsentimental outlook and his swiftly glancing free verse:

> No one to care there for Aneirin Lewis spilt there
> who worshipped his ancestors like a Chink
> who sleeps in Arthur's lap
> who saw Olwen-trefoils some moonlighted night
> on precarious slats at Festubert,
> on narrow foothold on le Plantin marsh—
> more shaved he is to the bare bone than
> Yspaddadin Penkawr.
> Properly organized chemists can make more riving
> power than ever Twrch Trwyth;
> more blistered he is than painted Troy Towers
> and unwholer, limb from limb, than any of them fallen at Catraeth
> or on the seaboard down, by Salisbury,
> and no maker to contrive his funerary song.
> And the little Jew lies next him
> cries out for Deborah his bride
> and offers for stretcher bearers
> gifts for their pains
> and walnut suites in his delirium
> from Grays Inn Road.

II. IMAGISTS AND D. H. LAWRENCE

In the years immediately preceding the First World War there was a group of poets in London working on principles almost diametrically opposed to those of the Georgians. The Georgians had assumed that there was still an upper middle class with a living poetic culture, and that it was possible by means of a few minor reforms to achieve a renewal of the classic English poetic tradition comparable with that effected by Dryden in the sixteen-sixties, by Wordsworth in the seventeen-nineties or by Tennyson in the eighteen-forties. The 'Imagists', although they were only minor poets, had the merit of perceiving and declaring that this was no no longer possible. They were the first true 'modernist' group in the sense that they no longer attempted to communicate with a general public of poetry lovers which had ceased to exist, but concentrated on searching for a means of expressing the modern consciousness for their own satisfaction and that of their friends. The pretence that humanity was steadily progressing towards the millennium was to be abandoned and the poets had to recognize that they were living in a new dark age of barbarism and vulgarity where the arts could only survive in small islands of culture, which was no longer the possession of a securely established social class but which had to be fashioned anew by a self-chosen *élite* that managed to escape the spiritual degradation of a commercialised world. This attitude seems at first sight very much like that of the 'tragic generation' of the 'nineties, with whom indeed the Imagists had definite connections, but actually it was different. The aesthetes of the 'nineties withdrew into their ivory tower because they hated the vulgarity of the contemporary world and wanted to lose themselves among beautiful fantasies. The Imagists, on the contrary, wanted to create a very precise and concentrated expression of a new sort of consciousness for which the traditional techniques were inadequate.

Their philosopher was Thomas Edward Hulme (1883–1917), who was killed while serving in the artillery on the Western Front. Hulme's essays and notes (with six short poems) were published under the title of *Speculations* in 1924, but in the years preceding the war he had influenced the Imagists through his articles in periodicals and his friendship with Ezra Pound. Hulme was the first English thinker to make a frontal attack on the liberal humanism which had been the foundation of English middle-class culture

since the Renaissance. His main contention was that the humanist
tradition was now moribund, and that art and philosophy in
Europe had to make a new start. Philosophy was to revert to something like scholasticism and art to something like the hieratic and
geometrical art of Ancient Egypt and Byzantium. This art was to
be based on the idea of original sin, the conception of man as a
very imperfect creature 'intrinsically limited but disciplined by
order' as opposed to the romantic view of man as 'an infinite
reservoir of possibilities'. The world was no longer to be regarded
as a glorious place with which man was naturally in harmony but
'a landscape with occasional oases. . . . But mainly deserts of dirt,
ash-pits of the cosmos, grass on ashpits'. This is a remarkable fore-
shadowing of Eliot's vision of the 'waste land'. Hulme contended
that there was 'no universal ego but a few definite persons gradually
built up'. He clearly looked forward to a period like the Dark Ages
when the values of ethics and religion and art would be the property
of a small *élite* in a barbarous world. In his essay on 'Romanticism
and Classicism' he pleads for a classical poetry founded on fancy
rather than imagination and foretells the coming of such a poetry:
'I prophesy that a period of dry, hard, classical verse is coming'.
'I think there is an increasing proportion of people who simply
can't stand Swinburne'.

Hulme's ideas are a good deal more interesting than the poems
of his imagist disciples. The chief of these was the American Ezra
Pound (1885–   ) who had settled in London and published a
series of volumes of verse beginning with *Personae* (1909). Pound
is a poet of real originality but his talent was overlaid by masses
of rather ill-digested learning. He started as a disciple of Browning
and Swinburne and some of his early poems even show the influence
of Kipling. Then he passed to study the Provençal trobadors from
whose works he produced a series of free translations. In the years
immediately preceding 1914 he was translating or rather adapting
Anglo-Saxon, Latin, Chinese and Japanese poetry. He was a bold
and tireless experimenter in metre and his most important contribution to the poetry of the crisis is perhaps to be found in his
development of an unrhymed 'free verse' which was neither the
sprawling quality of Whitman's metre nor the flatness of Arnold's
unrhymed lyrics. He probably owed something to Henley and his
experiments certainly had an important effect on the work of
T. S. Eliot.

Pound was the presiding spirit of the group which produced the
anthology called *Des Imagistes* in 1914. This rather dilettante and

precious collection includes work by the English poets F. S. Flint, Richard Aldington and F. M. Hueffer, the Irishman James Joyce and the Americans Ezra Pound, Allen Upward, H. D. (Hilda Doolittle), Amy Lowell and William Carlos Williams. The strong American element in the Imagist group is significant. The tradition of middle-class culture was much weaker in America than in England and was being swamped by the great influx of immigrants. It was therefore natural that American poets should reject it sooner than their English counterparts.

Instead of imitating the English romantics like the Georgians, the Imagists attempted to reproduce the qualities of Ancient Greek and Chinese poetry. They aimed at hard, clear, brilliant effects instead of the soft, dreamy vagueness or the hollow Miltonic rhetoric of the English nineteenth-century tradition. Their aims as expressed in *Some Imagist Poets* (1915) can be summarised as follows:

(1) To use the language of common speech, but to employ always the exact word, not the nearly exact, nor the merely decorative word.

(2) To produce poetry that is hard and clear, and not to deal in vague generalities, however magnificent and sonorous.

(3) To create new rhythms and not to copy old rhythms, which merely echo old moods.

These aims, though inadequate, were salutary as a protest against the hollow wordiness of much contemporary English poetry, its reliance on the jingle of rhyme and the mechanical quality of its metre. The Imagists, however, lived too much among books, were too self-consciously Bohemian, and lacked both fundamental brainwork and contact with contemporary actualities. They aimed at the clarity and concentration of the classic Chinese lyric and the Greek epigram but did not realise that these forms grew out of highly civilised societies in conditions which did not exist in early twentieth-century England. The result is that the neo-hellenism and *chinoiserie* of the Imagist anthologies now seem as faded and affected as the neo-romanticism of the Georgians. However, the Imagists are to be commended for showing that English poetry needed a new technique and, as Edwin Muir has written, for 'removing unnecessary rules and a burdensome mass of dead associations'. Imagism was only one phase in Pound's career. He passed on to a direct satire on the modern world in 'Hugh Selwyn Mauberley' (1920), perhaps his best poem, which suffers, however, by comparison with T. S. Eliot's early writing, by which it is probably influenced. His 'Draft of XXX Cantos' designed to be the first instalment of his masterpiece is a vast jumbled mass, in which Social Credit, the Renaissance, Ancient Greece and China jostle each other without any apparent coherence. Unlike Yeats and Eliot, with both of whom he was intimate, Pound yielded to the attractions of fascism and became Mussolini's American mouthpiece in the Second World War.

The most notable writer directly connected with the Imagists is certainly David Herbert Lawrence (1885–1930). Lawrence, like Blake, with whom he has often been compared, is difficult to fit into any historical perspective. He contributed both to Georgian Poetry and the later Imagist anthologies, but he was neither a Georgian nor an Imagist. He was singularly unfortunate in his life and the period in which his genius developed. The son of a Nottinghamshire miner and an ambitious mother, he turned his back on his working-class world and became first a teacher and then a novelist and the husband of a divorced German baroness. Had he been born twenty or thirty years earlier in a period when Victorian society was still stable and possessed a really solid culture, Lawrence might have become a great regional author like Hardy in contact with the world of letters and scholarship and at the same time drawing strength from a local folk tradition. Unfortunately he grew up in a period of confusion when the old class structure of English life was collapsing in the years immediately preceding the First World War. The war turned him into a kind of pariah, and he suffered bitter humiliation on account of his German wife and because he was rejected as physically unfit for military service. At the same time his passionate and frank (but never ignoble) treatment of sexual themes in a series of magnificent works of prose fiction exposed him to a stupid puritanical outcry, and caused several of his books to be banned, thus turning him into an isolated and embittered man.

He described himself as a 'passionately religious man'. In his youth he had lost his belief in the Puritan Christianity of his ancestors but he made a kind of religion for himself which he imagined to have been the primitive religion of mankind. This was a belief in 'dark gods' who were the representatives of the 'blood' as opposed to the intellect. In his later years he was haunted by a notion of finding remains of this primitive religion and culture, and also of building up a community which should be free from the ugliness and spiritual degradation of commercialised 'civilisation'. The quest for this ideal 'natural' life drove him on a series of pilgrimages to Ceylon, Australia and finally New and Old Mexico.

In the preface to his *Collected Poems* Lawrence wrote that most of his early verses 'in their fragmentary fashion . . . make up a biography of an emotional and inner life'. They represent a long, difficult 'voyage within' undertaken with the courage and determination of a poet who was one of the great life-adventurers of his age. He started by writing verse in the rhyming forms of the Georgians, but, unlike theirs, his early nature poems are full of sharp personal sensations, almost painful in their intensity. The transition from this beautiful but essentially minor poetry of his youth to his major achievements in verse is seen in the memorable sequence of lyrics called *Look We Have Come Through* (1917). The complexity of Lawrence's earlier emotional experience is now simplified into a kind of duel of sex, a 'conflict of love and hate' between man and wife. The sequence is a true voyage of discovery in the world of the spirit leading to an exciting culmination in a group of poems that express an annihilation of the ego and a sort of mystical rebirth or regeneration. The remarkable poem 'Manifesto' ends with a vision of a universe where all human beings have completely realised their individualities, where

> all men detach themselves and become unique
> . . . .
> Every human being will then be like a flower, untrammelled,
> Every movement will be direct.
> Only to be will be such delight, we cover our faces when we think of it
> Lest our faces betray us to some untimely fiend.

Lawrence had now developed a peculiar kind of free verse which owes something to Whitman and probably also the Old Testament poetry in which he had been steeped in his youth. In this form he wrote the collection of poems called *Birds, Beasts and Flowers* (1923) which represents the full flowering of his poetic genius freed from the autobiographical preoccupation. Here he gives notable expression to that awareness of 'unknown modes of being' which is, perhaps, his most signal contribution to English poetry. His 'Snake' in this collection is both a memorable exploration of a life different from that of a humanity and a profound criticism of the world of 'civilisation':

> He lifted his head from his drinking, as cattle do,
> And looked at me vaguely, as drinking cattle do,
> And flickered his two-forked tongue from his lips, and mused a moment

And stooped and drank a little more,
Being earth-brown, earth-golden from the burning bowels of the earth
. . . he seemed to me again like a king,
Like a king in exile, uncrowned in the underworld,
Now due to be crowned again.

When Lawrence was dying of consumption in the South of France
in the spring of 1930, he wrote a handful of poems which deal
with the themes of death and eternity. Fragmentary as they are,
these last works of Lawrence, notably 'Bavarian Gentians', 'Shadows'
and 'The Ship of Death' have an intensity of vision and a tranquil
majesty of imagery and rhythm which give them a unique place
in modern English poetry, and suggest that, if Lawrence had lived
longer, he might have become a religious poet of a very high
order. Some of his poetry, like some of his fiction, suffers because
he was, in his own words, 'torn off from the body of mankind' and
lacked a social background and a tradition. Apart from his considerable contribution to the rebuilding of English poetry, the
importance of which is perhaps only beginning to be fully realised,
he played a notable part as a critic in clearing away the lumber of
dead traditions, and setting before English poets that salutary ideal
which he described in a famous letter:

The essence of poetry with us in this age of stark and unlovely
actualities is a stark directness, without a shadow of a lie, or a shadow of
deflection anywhere. Everything can go, but this stark, bare, rocky
directness of statement, this alone makes poetry, to-day.[1]

[1] Letter dated 11 June 1916. *Letters*, p. 308.

7

T. S. ELIOT

The important fact that every poet—and indeed every serious writer—had to face in England in the first half of the twentieth century was that the society in which he was living was in a very high degree hostile to the spiritual life. The poets up to and including the Georgians, had been writing as though no such hostility existed. Even when they were realistic and satiric, their work had been founded on the assumption that there was a class of 'common readers' with whom they could communicate, a class with a genuine culture and a real concern for spiritual values. The First World War in its later phases opened the eyes of poets like Sassoon, Owen and Rosenberg, who suddenly saw the modern world in all its naked horror unmasked by the impact of war, and were shocked into the creation of vital poetry. Conditions of life in the trenches in 1917–18, however, might be considered exceptional. If poetry was to regain its honesty, it would have to recognize the fact that the values of the old cultivated middle class (people like the Meyricks in *Daniel Deronda* or even the Schlegels in *Howards End*) were dead beyond recall, and that it was necessary to find expression for a new sort of sensibility arising out of conditions that were wholly different from those of the agricultural, class-dominated society from which the old traditions of English poetry had sprung. The result would necessarily be a poetry that would appear to many readers brought up in these traditions to be both 'unpleasant' and 'difficult'. It would appear to be unpleasant because contemporary society was in a state of progressive degradation, and if poetry was to be a true 'criticism of life' and a revelation of its essential nature, it had to express the horror of such a world, a horror from which the poets had, for the most part, averted their eyes, though it had been revealed in a different medium by a series of novelists from George Gissing to Joseph Conrad. The poets would have to immerse themselves in 'the destructive element'[1] as Conrad does in the following passage from *The Secret Agent* (1907):

In front of the great doorway, a dismal row of newspaper sellers standing clear of the pavement dealt out their wares from the gutter. It was a raw, gloomy day of the early Spring; and the grimy sky, the mud of the streets, the rags of the dirty men, harmonised excellently with the eruption of the damp, rubbishy sheets of paper soiled with printers' ink. The posters maculated with filth, garnished like tapestry the sweep of the curbstone. The trade in evening papers was brisk, yet in comparison with the swift, constant march of foot traffic the effect was of indifference, of a disregarded distribution.

Here the novelist has not merely reported the hideousness of the scene; he has even performed part of the poet's function of finding words to express his vision of the strange, grotesque beauty which is part of that hideousness. What he had not done (and, of course, could not do in the prose medium) was to find verse rhythms which would express the impact of such a scene on a person with a poetic sensibility.

A poet who attempted to make full use of such experiences, that is not merely to report them in competent traditional verse but to express their effect on his inner life would almost certainly be considered 'difficult' in a period when no traditional technique existed for this purpose. 'It appears likely', T. S. Eliot wrote in his essay on 'The Metaphysical Poets', 'that poets in our civilisation, as it exists at present, must be *difficult*. Our civilisation comprehends great variety and complexity, and this variety and complexity, playing upon a refined sensibility, must produce various and complex results. The poet must become more and more comprehensive, more allusive, more indirect, in order to force, to dislocate if necessary, language to his meaning'. The poets would, in fact, have to attempt the supremely difficult task or creating new poetic idioms and rhythms out of modern colloquial speech, suggestions

---

[1] The phrase is from Conrad's *Lord Jim* (1900), used effectively by I. A. Richards in his *Science and Poetry* (1926) and adopted by Stephen Spender as the title of his well-known critical work.

from older English poetry or the poetry of other nations. They would only be able to communicate with an *élite* consisting of readers who shared in some degree their own power of perceiving the aesthetic significance of the changes that were taking place in the contemporary world. This would have the advantage of enabling them to concentrate on the task of expression, but it would also have the drawback of making them, in some degree at any rate, exclusive, bookish and inhuman.

Much of the importance of the early work of Thomas Stearns Eliot (1888–1965) lies in the fact that he was the first English-speaking poet of genius who was fully aware of the implications of the new situation. Eliot had the advantage of being brought up in the tradition of English literary culture, and yet, at the same time, of being able to see it, as a foreigner sees it, from the outside. It was an advantage which could, perhaps, be only fully enjoyed by an American with a cosmopolitan education. On the other hand, his early life in America brought him into touch with a society which was probably even more corrupt and hostile to spiritual values than that of Europe. This was a disadvantage, because he thus acquired an excessive preoccupation with the staleness and flatness of modern life, as well as a kind of fastidious shrinking from its brutality and meanness, which colours much of his poetry.

Born at St Louis, Missouri, he came from a distinguished and highly cultivated New England family. In 1906 he entered Harvard University where he attracted attention as a writier of verse, and attended the lectures of George Santayana and Irving Babbitt. He spent 1910–11 in Paris studying French literature and philosophy at the Sorbonne; returning to America, he continued his study of philosophy at Harvard and also received some instruction in Sanskrit and Indian philology, spending 'a year in the mazes of Patanjali's meta-physics', which left him 'in a state of enlightened mystification'.[1] He went to Germany with a travelling scholarship in 1913, and, in the first year of the war, was studying philosophy at Merton College, Oxford. He now settled in England and his first mature poems were published in English periodicals in 1915–16. He taught for a time at Highgate School and afterwards worked in a London bank. In the years immediately following the war he was an active contributor to London literary periodicals. He founded and edited *The Criterion*, and became a director of the publishing firm of Faber and Faber. He was naturalised as a British

---

[1] *After Strange Gods*, p. 40.

subject in 1927, and in a volume of essays published in 1928 described his 'general point of view' as 'classicist in literature, royalist in politics and Anglo-Catholic in religion'.[1]

Eliot was closely connected with Ezra Pound and the Imagist group during the early years of his residence in London. His early poetry owes something to these writers but much more to his intensive study of the Elizabethan and Jacobean dramatists, the metaphysical poets of the seventeenth century, Baudelaire and French symbolists, and Dante. T. E. Hulme's attack on the liberal-humanist tradition and his plea for a 'dry, hard classical verse' also had an important effect on him and the writings of the French royalist Charles Maurras worked in a similar direction.

Eliot's first poems collected in the volume called *Prufrock and other Observations* (1917) are a landmark in English poetry because their author entirely abandons the pretence of entertaining and instructing an imaginary 'common reader' and concentrates instead on using every means in his power to express the 'boredom, the horror and the glory'[2] of the contemporary world. Here is a poet who has thoroughly immersed himself in the destructive element, the sordidness, the stupidity and the ugliness of modern urban life, without surrendering to its values, which he treats with the curiosity of an artist and the irony of a keenly critical intellect. He has made the 'voyage without' and the 'voyage within' in the spirit, not of a fugitive or a tourist in search of the picturesque but of an explorer. These poems convey an unforgettable impression of the presence of the great modern city, a hell even more terrible than the trench landscape of Wilfred Owen, because its misery is listless and undramatic:

> Let us go then, you and I,
> When the evening is spread out against the sky
> Like a patient etherised upon a table;
> Let us go, through certain half-deserted streets,
> The muttering retreats
> Of restless nights in one-night cheap hotels
> And sawdust restaurants with oyster-shells:
> Streets that follow like a tedious argument

---

[1] Preface to *For Lancelot Andrewes, Essays on Style and Order* (1928), p. ix. When this volume was reprinted in 1936 under the title *Essays Ancient and Modern*, the preface containing these words was omitted.
[2] *The Use of Poetry and the Use of Criticism* (1933), p. 106.

Of insidious intent
To lead you to an overwhelming question. . . .
O do not ask, 'What is it?'
Let us go and make our visit.

In the room the women come and go
Talking of Michelangelo.

Eliot, like Milton, is a poet whose earliest published works exhibit in embryo all the chief characteristics of his fully developed writings. There is a sense in which the whole of Eliot is in 'The Love Song of J. Alfred Prufrock' as there is a sense in which the whole of Milton is in the Nativity Ode. The writer of the lines quoted above has been to school with French symbolists, not so much with Mallarmé and Verlaine, the two poets who most influenced Yeats and his contemporaries of the 'tragic generation', as with Jules Laforgue and Tristan Corbière, writers who had evolved a peculiar technique based on the use of the rhythms of colloquial speech, imagery drawn from contemporary life and sudden transitions from lyric intensity to terse ironic realism. It is a technique which gets rid of much that was considered necessary when the poet was also a storyteller or a teacher. Eliot himself describes it excellently in an essay on another French writer:

Any obscurity on first reading is due to the suppression of 'links in the chain', of explanatory and connecting matter, and not to incoherence or to the love of cryptogram. The justification of such abbreviations of method is that the sequence of images coincides and concentrates into one intense impression.

The reader has to allow the images to fall into the memory successively without questioning the reasonableness of each at the moment; so that at the end a total effect is produced. Such a selection of images has nothing chaotic about it. There is a logic of imagination as well as a logic of concepts. . . .[1]

This method of writing depends very largely on the effective use of imagery. The poets who use it, as Dr. Bowra has said, 'need images to express the full complexity of their moods and use them more freely to convey the special thrill which they regard as their special function'.[2] Eliot, in his early poems is trying to

[1] Preface to translation of *Anabase* by St J. Perse (1930).
[2] C. M. Bowra, *The Creative Experiment*, p. 8.

convey not only moods but thought by means of imagery thus emulating that 'direct sensuous apprehension of thought, or . . . recreation of thought into feeling' that he admired in the English poetry of the early seventeenth century. Thus the thought of Prufrock's dumb agony is sensuously apprehended in the image of the evening as 'a patient etherised upon a table', the lazy animalism of life in the great city in the image of the yellow fog as a sleepy cat that 'rubs its back upon the window-panes' and 'licked its tongue into the corners of the evening', and Prufrock's desperation receives a terrifying visual form as

> a pair of ragged claws
> Scuttling across the floors of silent seas.

The two most important poems in the 1917 volume, 'The Love Song of J. Alfred Prufrock' and 'A Portrait of a Lady' are both closely related to the art of Henry James. Prufrock and the Lady are, in fact, typical Jamesian characters, lonely, sensitive, fastidious people like Milly Theale and Lambert Strether:

> Now that lilacs are in bloom
> She has a bowl of lilacs in her room
> And twists one in her fingers while she talks.
> 'Ah, my friend, you do not know, you do not know
> What life is, you hold it in your hands';
> (Slowly twisting the lilac stalks)
> 'You let it flow from you, you let it flow,
> And youth is cruel, and has no remorse
> And smiles at situations which it cannot see.'
> I smile, of course,
> And go on drinking tea.

This is what James in *The Art of Fiction* calls an 'incident': 'It is an incident', he writes, 'for a woman to stand up with her hand resting on a table and look at you in a certain way; or if it be not an incident, I think it will be hard to say what it is. At the same time it is an expression of character'. These poems, like much of Henry James's fiction, are built on the perception of the profound significance of apparently trivial events. But for Eliot this significance conveyed the thrill of poetry. In fact these poems may be described as the use of James's methods to express poetic experience.

The first phase of Eliot's poetry is concerned with living in hell, the grimy, squalid banal hell of modern urban life. 'Any life', he wrote in his essay on 'Imperfect Critics', 'if accurately and profoundly penetrated, is interesting and always strange.'[1] In such a poem as 'Rhapsody on a Windy Night' he found the right technique to effect an accurate and profound penetration of the dreariness of the great modern city. The staccato rhythms of the following lines represent a complete break with the fluid, harmonious movement which had characterised most serious English poetry since Spenser.

> Half past three,
> The lamp sputtered,
> The lamp muttered in the dark.
> The lamp hummed:
> 'Regard the moon,
> La lune ne garde aucune rancune,
> She winks a feeble eye,
> She smiles into corners.
> She smooths the hair of the grass.
> The moon has lost her memory.
> A washed-out smallpox cracks her face,
> Her hand twists a paper rose,
> That smells of dust and eau de Cologne,
> She is alone
> With all the old nocturnal smells
> That cross and cross across her brain' . . . .[2]

Nevertheless, in the volume of 1917 life in hell is treated with a certain ironic gaiety and gusto, a youthful cynicism which finds free play in such poems as the brilliant and amusing 'Mr Apollinax'. The author of these poems is, perhaps, the first important poet since Pope who can be described as witty. In a happier society than that of England in the second and third decades of the twentieth century this urbane observer and master of phrase might have achieved a synthesis of social satire with that grave beauty which finds expression in the perfect lyric which concludes the volume:

> Stand on the highest pavement of the stair—
> Lean on a garden urn—

[1] *The Sacred Wood* (1928), p. 31.
[2] Compare this passage with the lines on the moon by W. E. Henley quoted on p. 27.

Weave, weave the sunlight in your hair—
Clasp your flowers to you with a pained surprise—

The *Poems* of 1920 also contain much wit and humour, but they are more serious. 'Gerontion', which stands at the head of the collection, is Eliot's first great prophetic poem. It is also his first attempt to put into practice that ideal of 'tradition' in poetry which he expounds in his essay on 'Tradition and the Individual Talent'. 'Tradition' in the sense that Eliot uses the word has nothing to do with the traditional techniques of poetry. It involves, he writes, 'the historical sense, which we may call nearly indispensable to anyone who would continue to be a poet beyond his twenty-fifth year; and the historical sense involves a perception, not only of the pastness of the past, but of its presence; the historical sense compels a man to write not merely with his own generation in his bones, but with a feeling that the whole of the literature of Europe from Homer and within it the whole of the literature of his own country has a simultaneous existence and composes a simultaneous order'. The historical sense is further defined as 'a sense of the timeless as well as of the temporal and of the timeless and temporal together'. 'Tradition' in the sense defined here is the basis of all Eliot's mature poetry, and the method of expressing it is the 'logic of imagination' or the presentation of material not in the chronological sequence of direct narrative or in the sequence of conceptual logic but arranged so as to form what I. A. Richards called the 'music of ideas'. This method, already foreshadowed in 'The Love Song of J. Alfred Prufrock', is first used in the way which Eliot has made peculiarly his own in 'Gerontion', which may be described in Dr Johnson's phrase as 'the dawn or twilight' of *The Waste Land* and the *Four Quartets*.

The speaker in this poem is not a 'character' like Prufrock or the Lady; he is an impersonal symbol, European civilisation imaged as an old man full of memories, for whom Thermopylae and the war of 1914–1918 have 'a simultaneous existence'. Now he is 'a dull head among windy places', who no longer even owns the 'decayed house' where he lives, but is merely the tenant of a Jew 'spawned in some estaminet of Antwerp'. His world is dry, dead and uncreative—

Rocks, moss, stonecrop, iron, merds.

Yet he can remember the last great uprush of the spiritual life:

> In the juvescence[1] of the year
> Came Christ the tiger.
>
> In depraved May, dogwood and chestnut, flowering judas

This passage is an example of Eliot's power of finding language to explore and express obscure states of mind. The connections between religion and erotic experience, and between creative activity and decay which we all feel obscurely and which cannot be expressed in any merely rational form are admirably suggested by the image of Christ as a tiger coming into the world in the spring of a new age which is also the 'depraved' corruption of an old one. The whole passage with all its splendour is nevertheless an expression of that fear of life which was to be one of the central themes of *The Waste Land*. That fear is certainly a characteristic of the modern world, particularly of the world as it was in the years immediately following the Treaty of Versailles, but too often Eliot makes us feel that it is his own fear. He has 'immersed' himself so completely in 'the destructive element' that he is infected with its poison.[2]

The central passage of the poem has both a moral depth and an artistic solidity beyond anything that Eliot had previously written. It is in a blank verse based on the rhythms of the early seventeenth-century dramatists of whose works Eliot had been making a careful critical study. He has succeeded in reviving the tradition of abrupt, condensed writing which suits the expression of twentieth-century thought and emotion far better than the Spenserian tradition of gentle, fluid rhythm. Eliot not merely revives the blank verse rhythms of the Jacobean dramatist; he develops them so that in his hands they become something new with a genuine relationship to contemporary speech:

> After such knowledge, what forgiveness? Think now
> History has many cunning passages, contrived corridors
> And issues, deceives with whispering ambitions,

---

[1] My friend, the late Sir George Rostrevor Hamilton, in his book *The Tell Tale Article* (p. 41), has taken Eliot to task for this word, which he describes as a 'barbarism'. I disagree. The 'correct' form etymologically would certainly be 'juvenescence'; but 'juvescence' seems to me a happy invention, combining the idea of youth (*juvenis*) with that of enjoyment (*juvare*).

[2] I do not mean that he ever adopted the base moral values of the contemporary world, but that he portrays its fear and impotence with such intensity that he seems to share those qualities. It was only when he adopted a positive religious attitude that he freed himself from the infection.

Guides us by vanities. Think now
She gives when our attention is distracted
And what she gives, gives with such supple confusions
That the giving famishes the craving. Gives too late
What's not believed in, or if still believed,
In memory only, reconsidered passion. Gives too soon
Into weak hands, what's thought can be dispensed with
Till the refusal propagates a fear. Think
Neither fear nor courage save us. Unnatural vices
And fathered by our heroism. Virtues
Are forced upon us by our impudent crimes.

This passage is truly tragic in its insight into the essential evil of the temporal world and its grave pity for the victims of history. There is a tragic magnificence, too, in the conclusion, where, using a suggestion from Chapman's *Bussy d'Ambois*, Eliot shows ignoble representatives of modern urban life in violent juxtaposition with the clean, cold inhuman splendours of sky and sea:

De Bailhache, Fresca, Mrs Cammel, whirled
Beyond the circuit of the shuddering Bear
In fractured atoms. Gull against the wind, in the windy straits
Of Belle Isle, or running on the Horn,
White feathers in the snow.

Here is a cosmic sweep and grandeur of imagination which were new developments in Eliot's poetry, placing it in an entirely different class from that of Pound and the Imagists.

In the 1920 volume, Sweeney, one of Eliot's most remarkable creations, makes his first appearance. Founded apparently on memories of an Irish-American pugilist whom Eliot had known in his youth, this figure is the type of the modern lout, the grotesquely ugly and crassly unspiritual being produced by Western urban 'civilisation'. There is no bitterness in Eliot's portrayal of Sweeney. He is a kind of Yahoo, but a good-natured and even shrewd and sensible Yahoo. In 'Sweeney among the Nightingales' he is seen in a disreputable café into which sunlight is pouring through a window opening on to a garden full of flowers and nightingales. The stupidity and sordidness of the jaded, corrupt men and women in the café is contrasted not only with the beauty of birdsong, flowers and sunshine but with the grandeur of sea and sky and the magnificence of the past which they ignore, but which the poet's vision reveals in dramatic contrast with their pettiness:

The circles of the stormy moon
Slide westward toward the River Plate,
Death and the Raven drift above
And Sweeney guards the horned gate.
. . . .

The host with someone indistinct
Converses at the door apart,
The nightingales are singing near
The Convent of the Sacred Heart,

And sang within the bloody wood
When Agamemnon cried aloud,
And let their liquid siftings fall
To stain the stiff dishonoured shroud.

The classic beauty of the phrasing of this poem is perhaps the highest technical achievement of Eliot's early work but the collection of 1920 suffers by the continual dwelling on the contrast between the grandeur of the past and the meanness and ugliness of the present. 'Where are the eagles and the trumpets?' the poet asks in that delightful and amusing poem 'A Cooking Egg', and the answer is that they are 'Buried beneath some snow-deep Alps', while

Over buttered scones and crumpets
Weeping, weeping multitudes
Droop in a hundred A.B.C.'s.

It is as though Eliot's exploration of the inner life reaches a certain point but is arrested because he cannot tear himself away from the combined horror and fascination of his vision of the meanness and staleness of contemporary humanity.

All Eliot's early poetry converges on *The Waste Land* (1922). Here he was attempting a task of enormous difficulty and the remarkable measure of success which he achieved is one of the chief testimonies to his genius. *The Waste Land* is an essay in creating a poem on a grand scale out of a vision of a devitalised world, a world that has denied or ignored the spiritual life. He had already treated this theme on a small scale in 'Gerontion', but that poem has the quality of a brief tragic and satiric comment cast in the form of a dramatic monologue. In *The Waste Land* the problem was to create a myth that would give adequate expression to the pity and terror of a comprehensive view of a devitalised society. For this purpose Eliot makes use of the two typically modern sciences of psychology and anthropology. Translations of the writing of Sigmund Freud had attracted widespread interest in psycho-analysis and the psychology of sex in the years immediately following the First World War,[1] and they had already exercised considerable influence on writers such as James Joyce and D. H. Lawrence. The central conception of *The Waste Land* is sexual impotence used as a symbol for the spiritual malady of the modern world. This symbol is developed by means of a myth which had been much studied by contemporary anthropologists. This is the vegetation myth with the rites of fertility based upon it found in the Eastern cults described by Sir James Frazer in his *Attis, Adonis, Osiris* (1920), to which Eliot acknowledges a particular debt. The specific example of the myth which he selects is derived from the theory of Miss J. L. Weston, expounded in several of her books and notably in *From Ritual to Romance* (1920). Miss Weston's theory was that the story of the quest for the Holy Grail was a Christianised version of 'an ancient Ritual, having for its ultimate objects the initiation into the secret of the Sources of Life, physical and Spiritual'[2], in fact a ritual based on a vegetation myth of the same kind as the myth of Adonis and similar Eastern cults. The Grail romances tell of a waste land[3], ruled by a maimed and impotent Fisher King. The king is freed from his impotence and the land from its aridity by a deliverer (Gawain or Percival), who makes use of certain magical instruments, a lance or spear and the grail or sacred chalice, which clearly symbolise sexual activity. The old use of mythology either as a simple tale or an allegory was clearly impossible for a poet of Eliot's sophistication. He showed, however, that a modern poet could make effective use of mythology, with the help of the psychologist and the anthropologist.

The technique of the poem is that of 'the music of ideas' already attempted on a small scale in 'Gerontion'. Here it is organised with great skill and elaboration in five sections or movements, the first of which introduces the main themes, which are developed with variations in the second and third while the fourth is short, grave and slow, a kind of pause before an impressive culmination in the fifth.

The themes of this symphonic poem are a series of scenes rather

---

[1] English translations of Freud's *Interpretation of Dreams* appeared in 1913, of his *Psychopathology of Everyday Life* in 1914, of *Totem and Taboo* in 1919, and of the *Introductory Lectures* in 1922.

[2] *From Ritual to Romance*, p. 191.

[3] The title of *The Waste Land* actually comes from Miss Weston's book. See *From Ritual to Romance*, ch. II.

like film shots fading and dissolving into each other, seen from
the viewpoint of an impersonal observer, the protagonist of the
poem, who is identified with the impotent Fisher King and also
with Tiresias the blind prophet of Greek legend. In one of his
notes Eliot writes that Tiresias, 'although a mere spectator and
not indeed a "character", is yet the most important personage in
the poem, uniting all the rest. . . . What Tiresias *sees*, in fact, is
the substance of the poem'. Tiresias, like the Spirit of the Years in
The Dynasts, is an embodiment of the modern mind, the keen
observer who is 'powerless to act'.

In the first section of the poem this spectator is seen in a dry,
desolate place, the 'waste land' of the Grail Legend which is also
Ezekiel's 'valley of dry bones':

> Where the sun beats,
> And the dead tree gives no shelter, the cricket no relief,
> And the dry stone no sound of water.

In this desert there is a red rock which seems to symbolise poetic
inspiration. It is from the shadow of this red rock, the one refuge
in the desolation, that the spectator promises 'to show you fear
in a handful of dust'. This fear is both the fear of life, and, as F. R.
Leavis has suggested, 'A nameless, ultimate fear, a horror of the
completely negative; it is the horrible echo of the caves in *A Passage
to India* which proclaims that "everything exists, nothing has value"'.

Miss Weston has associated with the fertility rites the Tarot
pack or ancient set of playing cards used for divination. In the
first section of the poem Madame Sosostris the 'famous clairvoyante'
has one of these 'wicked packs', and she picks from them various
cards which are the starting points of subsequent developments in
the poem. These cards represent three archetypal figures with a
mysterious fourth in the background who never materialises,
represented by a blank card. There is the man with the three staves,
who is the Fisher King, or the poet himself; there is the woman
'Belladonna', 'the lady of situations' who appears as the rich
neurotic lady of the opening monologue and again in the gorgeous
romantic setting at the opening of the second section. She is the
poor prostitute in the pub at the end of the section, the typist
seduced by the house agent's clerk, and Elizabeth dallying with
Leicester in a splendid bygone age. She is seen for a moment in a
more attractive form as a radiant girl, 'the hyacinth girl' of the
first section:

—Yet when we came back, late, from the Hyacinth garden,
Your arms full, and your hair wet, I could not
Speak, and my eyes failed, I was neither
Living nor dead, and I knew nothing,
Looking into the heart of light. . . .

Then there is a male figure, the 'one-eyed merchant' of the
Tarot pack. He is Mr Eugenides, the cosmopolitan, probably
homosexual, Greek from Smyrna who 'melts into the Phoenician
sailor and is not wholly distinct from Ferdinand Prince of Naples'.
He is also apparently the carbuncular house-agent's clerk who
seduces the typist and the nobler but equally empty-hearted Leicester
dallying with Elizabeth on a gilded barge on the Thames. This male
figure ought to be the deliverer of the Fisher King; actually he
fails because he profanes the mysteries. Here Eliot is almost certainly
influenced by a tradition which Miss Weston found in one of the
Grail romances. This tradition told how certain maidens whe were
guardians of the Grail mysteries were ravished by a robber king
and his knights and after that outrage the land became waste.[1] So
all the incarnations of the male figure in *The Waste Land* fail because
they profane the mysteries of life through greed and loveless lust.
The final failure is Phlebas, the Pheonician sailor who meets the
'death by water' prophesied by the clairvoyante. He had an eye for
the gulls and the sea swell but he thought too much of profit and
loss and this may be considered as a symbol of modern commercialism, whose arid spirit cannot endure the flood of passion.
Just as behind all the women is the Hyacinth Girl, the unrealised
promise of womanhood, so behind all the men is the image of the
true prince, Ferdinand of Naples suggested by the line quoted
from Shakespeare's lyric in the first section:

Those are pearls that were his eyes.

Ferdinand suffered a sea change into something rich and strange,
a rebirth through the power of love in Shakespeare's myth, but
in the modern world he is only a vague memory: Madame Sosostris
significantly cannot find 'The Hanged Man' among the cards; this
is the Hanged God of Frazer, and the implication is that the modern
world has lost its faith in Christ though it is still aware of His
presence, 'the third who always walks beside you' in the fifth
section.

---

[1] See *From Ritual to Romance*, pp. 162-3.

The whole poem is dominated by the nightmare vision of the great modern city:

> Unreal City,
> Under the brown fog of a winter dawn,
> A crowd flowed over London Bridge, so many,
> I had not thought death had undone so many,
> Sighs, short and infrequent, were exhaled,
> And each man fixed his eyes before his feet,
> Flowed up the hill and down King William Street,
> To where St Mary Woolnoth kept the hours
> With a dead sound on the final stroke of nine.

The effect of this passage is greatly enhanced by the knowledge that the fourth line is a translation of a line of Dante describing the lost souls in hell. There are dozens of such literary allusions in *The Waste Land*. Sometimes they are literal quotations and sometimes passages from older authors, wittily altered and distorted. Eliot's reading is part of his poetic experience and he uses it as freely as sensuous imagery. Effective as this use of pastiche is in many places, as in the passage quoted above, there is so much of it in *The Waste Land* that it becomes a mannerism and Eliot cannot be wholly acquitted of overloading his poem with recondite learning, a fault due perhaps to the influence of Ezra Pound, to whom the poem is dedicated. The introduction in the last section of Sanskrit words which have to be explained in the notes can hardly be defended.

Such faults, however, detract little from the overwhelming effect of the poem as a whole. In a sense it is fragmentary but this is because it expresses a vision of a fragmentary world. It is like a great picture of a city in ruins where the jagged outlines of the shattered buildings all contribute to a convincing organic pattern. It has been said that there is no development in *The Waste Land*, and it is true that, at the end of the poem, the vision of a parched and sterile world presented in the first section remains unchanged, or rather is presented with an even more terrifying intensity:

> There is not even silence in the mountains
> But dry sterile thunder without rain
> There is not even solitude in the mountains
> But red sullen faces sneer and snarl
> From doors of mudcracked houses. . . .

Nevertheless there is a real progression from the meaningless world of the bored rich woman ('What shall we ever do?') and the equally meaningless world of the woman in the pub ('Hurry up please it's time') to the grave tenderness of 'Death by Water':

> Gentile or Jew
> O you who turn the wheel and look to windward,
> Consider Phlebas, who was once handsome and tall as you,

and the apocalyptic quality of 'What the Thunder said'. The world remains parched and uncreative at the end of the poem but it is not meaningless. On the contrary the thunder (reinforcing the evidence of the Buddha and St Augustine) proclaims that the universe has a meaning and is founded on the eternal morality of 'give, sympathise, control'. It is true that no hope for the future is even hinted at, and at the end the poet can only 'shore against his ruins' fragments of verse representing the glories of European culture. Yet the implication is undoubtedly that humanity is condemned to a living death because it has disobeyed the eternal moral law and profaned the divine mysteries. So far from being poetry severed 'from all beliefs' as I. A. Richards suggested,[1] the poetry of *The Waste Land* is based on a very strong belief in original sin and the values of religion. Eliot's 'voyage within' has taken him as far as the negative side of religion: it was almost inevitable that he should proceed from this point to positive religious belief.

Eliot's journey into hell was continued after *The Waste Land* in two other poems. The first, 'The Hollow Men' (1925) is a much slighter and a much more personal poem than *The Waste Land*. The motto is 'a penny for the old guy' and modern humanity is seen as 'stuffed men' with 'headpiece filled with straw!' They have no eyes and their eyelessness is contrasted with the eyes which are a symbol of the life of the spirit imaged in a passage of delicate lyrical beauty:

> Sunlight on a broken column
> There, is a tree swinging
> And voices are
> In the wind's singing
> More distant and more solemn
> Than a fading star.

The 'hollow men' live in a world like that of the 'waste land', a

---

[1] I. A. Richards, *Science and Poetry*, p. 64.

dead, dry place of rats and broken glass. In this world there are no eyes, only a vague hope of recovering sight after death, though this is dismissed:

> The hope only
> Of empty men.

The poem ends with the famous lines that express with Eliot's peculiar terse, ironical wit the dull helplessness of Western Europe in the nineteen-twenties:

> *This is the way the world ends*
> *This is the way the world ends*
> *This is the way the world ends*
> *Not with a bang but a whimper.*

The final poem of Eliot's Inferno is the last and by far the most powerful of the Sweeney sequence. This is 'Sweeney Agonistes' (1926–27) consisting of two 'Fragments of an Aristophanic Melodrama' written in a jaunty rhyming verse from which both the lyrical beauty and the prophetic grandeur of Eliot's other major poems are completely excluded. The scene is a London flat where two prostitutes entertain some officers and American business men and finally Sweeney himself, who appears in the second fragment with his peculiar combination of grossness, vulgarity, good nature and clear and penetrating insight. The jazz songs in the second fragment are such close imitation of contemporary jazz songs that, as Stephen Spender writes, 'the parody becomes the thing parodied':

> *Tell me in what part of the wood*
> *Do you want to flirt with me?*
> *Under the breadfruit, banyan, palmleaf*
> *Or under the bamboo tree?*
> *Any old tree will do for me*
> *Any old wood is just as good*
> *Any old isle is just my style. . . .*

The sentimental inanity of the jazz song is perfectly caught in these lines but it needs the acuteness of Sweeney to reveal the inner meaning of the world that has produced this sort of pseudo-poetry. Doris, the corrupt townbred girl, cannot endure the thought of the 'life close to Nature' praised in the song. 'I'd be bored', she says, and Sweeney agrees, explaining that 'all the facts, when you come to brasstacks' are 'birth and copulation and death'. In exasperation she cries:

> That's not life, that's no life
> Why I'd just as soon be dead.

This gives Sweeney his cue:

> That's what life is. Just is.
>
> Doris: What is?
>
> What's that life is?
>
> Sweeney: Life is death.

This is the final point reached by Eliot in his exploration of 'the destructive element'. On the title page of *Sweeney Agonistes* he placed the saying of St John of the Cross: 'Hence the soul cannot be possessed of divine union, till it has divested itself of the love of created beings'. The 'love of created beings' if pursued exclusively leads finally to a life like that of Doris, Dusty and their pals, which is indistinguishable from death. It is a condemnation of the whole humanist tradition which began with the lofty visions of the Renaissance and ended with the corruption and boredom of the cities of the twentieth century.

Up to this point Eliot had been exploring both the outer and the inner worlds simultaneously, though, as I have already suggested, his 'voyage within' was checked by his disgust at the hideousness and stupidity which he found in the decaying civilisation around him. In the years following his conversion to Anglicanism he was able to continue the 'voyage within' more successfully because he was released from the nightmare vision of the modern world that haunted his earlier poetry, and also from the armour of irony which he had worn to protect himself from its contagion.

After 1926 or 1927 he began to write a new sort of poetry which seems to represent a withdrawal from the outer world and an exploration of the inner life under the guidance of Christianity. The new poetry begins with the *Ariel Poems*, 'The Journey of the Magi' (1927), 'A Song for Simeon' (1928), 'Animula' (1928) and the touching personal poem 'Marina' (1930). Side by side with these introspective poems Eliot was also writing some powerful social criticism in verse such as that remarkable satire on dictatorship, 'Coriolan'. The pageant play, *The Rock* (1934), was written for a special occasion and, taken as a whole, is not of permanent importance, but its choruses contain some of Eliot's most memorable poetry. Here are lyrics of grave beauty in flowing majestic rhythms (probably influenced by the Authorised Version of the Bible and the English Prayer Book) alternating with devastating ironic comment on the England of the age of Baldwin and Ramsay Macdonald:

> A Cry from the North, from the West, and from the South
> Whence thousands travel daily to the timekept City;
> Where My Word is unspoken,
> In the land of lobelias and tennis flannels
> The rabbit shall burrow and the thorn revisit,
> The nettle shall flourish on the gravel court,
> And the wind shall say: 'Here were decent godless people:
> Their only monument the asphalt road
> And a thousand lost golf balls.'

Ash Wednesday (1930) was Eliot's first considerable poem written after his conversion. It has connections with *The Waste Land*, but remarkable changes have taken place. Sweeney, Mrs Porter and their life, together with all the dull horror of the 'unreal city' have disappeared. Tiresias, the depersonalised observer, has gone and so have the smartness and literary parodies of the earlier poems. Instead there is a new austere humility:

> Because I do not hope to turn again
> Because I do not hope
> Desiring this man's gift and that man's scope
> I no longer strive to strive towards such things. . . .

The poem alternates between passages which seem to show the poet praying in 'a place of solitude', a desert like that of *The Waste Land* (but now freed from its nightmare atmosphere) and others in which his prayer is answered by a vision of a lady, perhaps symbolising the Church, called the 'veiled sister', who is associated with the life-giving waters for which he had cried in vain in *The Waste Land* and also with a garden which is the opposite to the parched desert of the earlier poem. The third section describes the ascent of a staircase, on the lower levels of which there are hideous images, 'the devil of the stairs' and darkness 'like an old man's mouth drivelling'. Then 'at the first turning of the third stair' through a slotted window there appears a vision of a spring landscape with a 'broadbacked figure drest in blue and green

F

playing on 'an antique flute', who is connected with memories
that recall 'La Figlia Che Piange' and *The Waste Land*:

> Blown hair is sweet, brown hair over the mouth blown,
> Lilac and brown hair. . . .

There is a further sense of terrible effort and then a tranquil vision
of the Lady in the garden in the fourth section:

> Who walked between the violet and the violet
> Who walked between
> The various ranks of varied green
> Going in white and blue, in Mary's colour.

The lady is seen 'behind the garden god', who is apparently the
'broadbacked figure' of the preceding section symbolising natural
beauty. Religion is thus somehow to restore the lost vision of
childhood, and the theme of the latter part of the section is the
redemption of the past:

> But the fountain sprang up and the bird sang down
> Redeem the time, redeem the dream
> The token of the word unheard, unspoken. . . .

The poem ends with a note of quiet wisdom, a kind of rule of life,
which was to be repeated again and again with variations in
Eliot's later works:

> Blessèd sister, holy mother, spirit of the fountain,
>   spirit of the garden,
> Suffer us not to mock ourselves with falsehood
> Teach us to care and not to care
> Teach us to sit still
> Even among these rocks,
> Our peace in His will. . . .

The 'Journey of the Magi' and 'A Song for Simeon' are religious
poems from which the tender sentiment of traditional Christian
verse is rigidly excluded, and replaced by an austerity that owes
something to Eliot's study of the sermons of Lancelot Andrewes.
These poems are full of a sense of effort and weariness. For this
poet religion is no sudden glory as it was for Hopkins but a hard

and difficult path of patience and renunciation:

> This set down
> This: were we led all that way for
> Birth or Death? There was Birth, certainly,
> We had evidence and no doubt. I had seen birth and death.
> But had thought they were different; this Birth was
> Hard and bitter agony for us, like Death, our death.

As all Eliot's early poetry converges on *The Waste Land*, all his later poetry converges on the *Four Quartets*, that remarkable sequence of poems which appeared between 1939 and 1942 (collected edition, 1943). The 'music of ideas', used in *The Waste Land* in a way that suggests the symphonic poem, here, as the title implies, finds embodiment in a form anologous to the sonata or the string quartet in its sudden changes of movement and complex interweaving of themes. 'Each poem,' writes an able critic,[1] 'is built up of five parts or movements with statement, counter-statement and resolution chasing one another throughout. A meditative movement usually executed in long loose-fibred lines of *vers libre*, is succeeded by a lyric, which in its turn is followed within the same movement by a further meditation. The third and fifth movements are again meditative (the lines at the end of the fifth being tautened with a shorter measure) while in between them is a short fourth movement consisting entirely of a lyric'. The form of the *Quartets* is one of Eliot's greatest artistic achievements; it is subtler, more complex and more controlled than that of any of his preceding works. The subject had already been hinted at in the fourth section of *Ash Wednesday*. It is time, its relation to the timeless and the 'redemption' of time. Two fragments of the early Greek philosopher Herakleitos are quoted on the title page. One suggests the famous Heraclitean doctrine of flux, the constant interchange between the four elements of air, earth, water, and fire between life and death. This interchange can be regarded as a 'way up', but, since according to Herakleitos it is a cyclic movement, it can equally be regarded as a 'way down'. The other fragment refers to Herakleitos's doctrine of the logos or directive intelligence behind the eternal flux, an intelligence with which human reason and language is connected. This doctrine has an obvious affinity to Christian teaching. These fragments are the key to the design of Eliot's sequence. Each of the four poems is a medita-

---

[1] Father E. J. Stormon S.J. in *Meanjin Papers III*, 2 (Brisbane 1949).

tion arising out of a certain locality associated with one of the four
Heraclitean elements and an aspect of human life which it symbolises. It is significant that none of these localities is urban. The
presence of the great modern city is indeed felt throughout the
sequence, but it is not haunting and oppressive as in *The Waste
Land;* it is seen, as it were, from the peaceful viewpoint of the
English countryside or the American coast.

The scene of the first quartet is Burnt Norton, a Gloucestershire
garden associated with the element of air and the beauty of childhood, of the second, East Coker, a Somersetshire village, the home
of Eliot's English ancestors, associated with earth and the seasons,
growth and decay. The third is named after the Dry Salvages, a
group of rocks on the Massachusetts coast, suggesting the element
of water, symbol of the eternal flux of time, while Little Gidding,
the scene of the fourth and culminating quartet, is the village
remembered as the home of Nicholas Ferrar the devout seventeenth-
century Anglican, friend of George Herbert and Richard Crashaw.
Its element is fire, symbol of love and religious devotion and it is
associated with history.

In each quartet there is a contrast between life in time and
'the timeless moment' or the 'point of intersection' of the timeless
with time, which can be regarded as the intervention of the Logos
of Herakleitos or Christ the Word of Christian theology. The main
theme of the whole sequence can be described as paradise regained.

Paradise is glimpsed in 'Burnt Norton' as 'the unheard music
hidden in the shrubbery', the 'leaves . . . full of children'. It is
contrasted with a 'place of disaffection', suggesting a London tube:

> Men and bits of paper, whirled by the cold wind
> That blows before and after time,
> Wind in and out of unwholesome lungs
> Time before and time after.
> Eructation of unhealthy souls
> Into the faded air, the torpid
> Driven on the wind that sweeps the gloomy hills of London, . . .

This contrast is developed in different ways in each of the succeeding
quartets and it is interwoven with the theme of old age. In his
demand for a heroic and adventurous old age Eliot is close to the
Yeats of 'Sailing to Byzantium'.

In 'East Coker' the redemption of time becomes the work of
Christ, whose intervention in the world of humanity is the subject
of a powerful lyric made up of paradoxes in the manner of Donne:

> The wounded surgeon plies the steel
> That questions the distempered part;
> Beneath the bleeding hands we feel
> The sharp compassion of the healer's art
> Resolving the enigma of the fever chart.

In the 'Dry Salvages' the words of Krishna to Arjuna in the Bhagavadgita bidding him go forward to the battle become an invigorating call to accept life:

> Not fare well,
> But fare forward, voyagers.

In the last movement of this quartet the vain desire to know the future through divination by astrology, palmistry and similar 'pastimes and drugs' is contrasted with the true apprehension of the timeless:

> But to apprehend
> The point of intersection of the timeless
> With time, is an occupation for the saint—
> No occupation either, but something given
> And taken in a lifetime's death in love,
> Ardour and selflessness and self-surrender.

This is the central doctrine of the sequence. The apprehension of the timeless can only be achieved through 'death in love', the Christian sacrifice. In 'Little Gidding', the deserted Chapel of the Ferrar community recalls the conflict of the seventeenth century, and the nobility of the two parties is symbolised by Charles I, the 'king at nightfall' who came to Little Gidding after the final defeat at Naseby, with his faithful followers, 'three men, and more, on the scaffold', and the Republicans 'a few who died forgotten' with their great poet Milton,

> one who died blind and quiet, ...

This is history, and history, rightly regarded, is freedom, the achievement of the timeless by a nation:

> Here, the intersection of the timeless moment
> Is England and nowhere. Never and always.

But history is not only the past. It is alive in the London of the

air raids of the Second World War. The scene of the memorable
second movement of the sequence is set in a London street just
before dawn after a raid, where the poet meets a 'familiar com-
pound ghost', who, speaking in rhythms that recall the movement
of the *Divine Comedy*, reveals the pity and terror of old age and the
means by which they can be overcome:

> Let me disclose the gifts reserved for age
>   To set a crown upon your lifetime's effort.
>   First, the cold friction of expiring sense
> Without enchantment, offering no promise
>   But bitter tastelessness of shadow fruit
>   As body and soul begin to fall asunder.
> Second, the conscious impotence of rage
>   At human folly, and the laceration
>   Of laughter at what ceases to amuse.
> And last, the rending pain of re-enactment
>   Of all that you have done, and been; the shame
>   Of motives late revealed, and the awareness
> Of things ill done and done to others' harm
>   Which once you took for exercise of virtue.
>   Then fools' approval stings, and honour stains
> From wrong to wrong the exasperated spirit
>   Proceeds, unless restored by that refining fire
>   Where you must move in measure, like a dancer.

The 'refining fire' is 'the flame of incandescent terror' celebrated
in the glowing lyric which is the fourth movement, and representing
the achievement of the 'timeless moment', the regaining of the
paradise of the first sequence:

> The voice of the hidden waterfall
> And the children in the apple-tree.

In the *Four Quartets* Eliot has in a sense overcome the 'schism in
the soul' and found a solution for the modern crisis but it is a
highly personal solution like that of Yeats in his later poems. Like
Paradise Regained, the *Four Quartets* is a poem for the few, moving
in an atmosphere of rarefied thought and feeling.

It is dangerous to draw critical conclusions from the work of a
poet whose career is still unfinished.[1] However, to the present
writer it seems that the *Four Quartets*, like *The Waste Land*, marks a

---

[1] This and the following paragraph were written in 1951.

definite stage in Eliot's development, the end of that period of withdrawal from the outer world that began with the *Ariel Poems* and *Ash Wednesday*. Will Eliot, strengthened by his retreat into the spiritual life, return to a new exploration of the outer world? The answer to this question may be found in his work for the theatre. The poet of 'The Love Song of J. Alfred Prufrock' and *The Waste Land* and above all 'Sweeney Agonistes' was obviously a potential dramatist and the author of *A Dialogue on Dramatic Poetry* (1928) had very clear ideas about the kind of poetic drama which ought to be written in the twentieth century. His two highly successful plays, *Murder in the Cathedral* (1935) and *The Family Reunion* (1939) are extremely suggestive experiments in a new kind of poetic drama uniting symbolism, realism and lyrical beauty. In these plays Eliot has rejected the old humanistic tradition of the drama of character which goes back to the Elizabethans, and produced a poetic drama which has affinities both to Greek tragedy and the late medieval morality plays. If this experiment is continued, and a theatre is found for dramas that are both effective acting plays and explorations of the spiritual life, it is possible that Eliot may have a very important part to play in that widening of the appeal of English poetry which will be its great task in the second half of the twentieth century.[1]

Even if his work had ceased with the *Four Quartets*, he would be remembered as one of the great renovators of English poetry. He has given it a new intellectual dignity, new forms arising out of a new sincerity and a new spiritual depth. Like Dryden after the Restoration and Wordsworth at the end of the eighteenth century he has also given it a new policy. More than any other poet he has saved it from becoming a mere pastime of the scholarly section of the upper middle class, like Latin poetry in the days of Claudian and Ausonius. His policy has been to write for poets and the small *élite* in modern England which takes poetry seriously. This was a dangerous policy because it was liable to lead to the vices of esotericism, bookishness and culture snobbery. It was, however, infinitely preferable to the other alternatives of euthanasia in a dead upper middle class tradition or surrender to the vulgarity of the crowd. Eliot's courage and integrity and fine critical sense

---

[1] The following statement from the conclusion of *The Use of Poetry and the Use of Criticism* (1933) seems to be highly significant in this connection: 'I believe the poet naturally prefers to write for as large and miscellaneous an audience as possible, and that it is the half-educated and ill-educated, who stand in his way. I myself should like to write for an audience which could neither read nor write'. op. cit. p. 152.

have enabled him in a large measure to avoid these dangers, though they have not always been avoided by this disciples. It was very fortunate for English poetry that the poet who carried out this great revolution is also one of the most acute and far-seeing of English critics.

AFTER ELIOT

I

The period between the two World Wars falls into two well defined sections. The first lasting till about 1929 was an age of confusion, bewilderment and disillusion. The high hopes for the future of mankind inspired by the utterances of President Wilson and other Allied statesmen were shattered by the realities of an exhausted and impoverished Europe where life nearly everywhere was shabbier and more dangerous than it had been in 1914. The United States withdrew from European affairs, repudiated the idealism of Wilson and refused to join the newly born League of Nations. Confused fighting went on in Russia and Eastern Europe for several years after the armistice of 1918, and, when the peace treaties had been signed, the former Allied countries with the newly established and still partly ostracised Soviet Union settled down to play the old game of power politics as cynically as if the 'war to end wars' had never been fought and the League of Nations had never existed. In England the short post-war trade boom was succeeded by a steadily increasing depression, accompanied by a rapid rise in the number of unemployed and numerous strikes and lockouts, leading up to the General Strike of 1926 and the economic crisis of 1929-30.

The second period begins with the collapse of American prosperity, the spreading of the great slump to Europe, followed by the Japanese aggression against China, the rise of the Nazi dictatorship, the re-arming of Germany, and the division of the world into fascist and anti-fascist camps, culminating in the Munich crisis of 1938 and the outbreak of the Second World War in 1939.

'In the nineteen-twenties', writes Stephen Spender, 'there was a tragedy to ignore or accept, but there seemed nothing to fight for or against. The revolutions which took place in Europe had the appearance of volcanoes, eruptions of despair and barbarism in the minds and bodies of the masses pouring out like lava over the cities. Besides this, the prevailing mood of the intellectuals who had known or been opposed to the war was one of political pacifism, a conviction that armed remedies can do no good'.[1]

The disintegration of the old structure of English society which had started in the years preceding the war was greatly accelerated. The old ruling class emerged from the war with greatly depleted incomes. Many of its members had to go into business or ally themselves with business magnates. Many of their town houses were turned into flats or offices and numerous great country houses were converted into schools, hotels, or convalescent homes. Ex-officers were glad to get jobs as salesmen for distributors of motor cars and many of them were compelled to tramp the streets and hawk goods from door to door. The plight of the D.S.O. in Somerset Maugham's play,[2] who tries to run a small garage and fails, was a common one, and the words which Maugham puts into the mouth of Sydney Ardsley represent very well the bitterness of thousands of ex-servicemen who were disgusted by the appalling waste of human material involved in the attempt of the post-war governments to put the clock back to 1914:—

I know that we were the dupes of the incompetent fools who ruled the nations. I know that we were sacrificed to their vanity, their greed and their stupidity. And the worst of it is that as far as I can tell they haven't learnt a thing. They're just as vain, they're just as greedy, they're just as stupid as ever they were. They muddle on, muddle on, and one of these days, they'll muddle us all into another war.

A few writers like T. S. Eliot and E. M. Forster could visualise the condition of this decaying society in terms of tragedy. The prevailing attitude, however, was the cynical pessimism of Aldous Huxley's *Antic Hay* (1923):

Long expected one-and-twenty has made me a fully privileged citizen of the great realm of which the owners of the *Daily Mirror*, the *News of the World*, and the *Daily Express* are noble peers. . . .

It's not the architecture I mind so much. . . . What disgusts me is the people inside the architecture, the number of them. . . . And the way

[1] 'The Life of Literature III', in *Partisan Review*, January 1949.
[2] *For Services Rendered.*

they breed. . . . like maggots. Millions of them creeping about the face of the country, spreading blight and dirt wherever they go. . . .

In this bewildered and decaying society the old literary conventions and standards had little chance of survival. Sir Edward Marsh wisely decided to discontinue *Georgian Poetry* after the appearance of a fifth volume in 1922. The 'Georgian' tradition was continued by J. C. Squire, a clever parodist and minor Georgian poet, who founded *The London Mercury* in 1919. The *Mercury*, which continued publication up to the eve of the Second World War, was respectable but dull. Distinguished elder poets like Hardy, Yeats, Bridges, Belloc and Kipling contributed to it, but it opposed or ignored the new movements in poetry. Its standards can be judged by an editorial statement which bracketed 'Yeats, Masefield, Kipling and Bridges' as the 'best living exponents of verse'.

Apart from certain gifted individuals such as James Joyce living in exile on the Continent, D. H. Lawrence wandering on his Savage Pilgrimage in the Mediterranean lands, Ceylon, Australia and New Mexico, and T. S. Eliot, patiently building up the delicate fabric of his art in London, there were two important centres of creative literary activity in the England of the nineteen-twenties. One was the group of writers and artists living near the British Museum, which came to be called 'Bloomsbury', and the other was the family party of the three Sitwells.

The Bloomsbury group included certain brilliant prose writers such as E. M. Forster, Virginia and Leonard Woolf, Lytton Strachey and Clive Bell, who rejected the realism of the late Victorian and Edwardian novel, the tradition of romanticism in poetry and of solemnity in biography and criticism. They had close connections with the two ancient universities and also with literary and artistic movements on the Continent. They admired French and Russian literature, and particularly the Anglo-French culture of the eighteenth century. They were humane and tolerant, and performed great services to English culture by re-examining critical aims and principles with a notable intellectual integrity, by opening up the English mind to French influences, especially French poetry and painting, and by the encouragement and help which they gave to young writers. The members of the Bloomsbury group wrote little verse, but they were interested in poetry and stimulated young poets.

The Sitwells were the three remarkable children of Sir George

Sitwell, a learned and eccentric Derbyshire baronet. They all wrote distinguished verse and prose, but Edith Sitwell (1887-1964) will probably be remembered as a major poet, Osbert (now Sir Osbert Sitwell, 1892–   ) as a brilliant novelist, satirist and auto-biographer, and Sacheverell (1897–   ) as a writer of imaginative art criticism and delicate fantasy in verse and prose. Like 'Blooms-bury', they were in close touch with Continental, and especially French movements in literature and art. They made their first public appearance as poets in the anthology called *Wheels*, six 'Cycles' of which, edited by Edith Sitwell, appeared between 1916 and 1921. *Wheels* was a deliberate challenge to *Georgian Poetry* and the Sixth Cycle contains a direct satiric attack on J. C. Squire and his friends by Augustine Rivers.

Like *Georgian Poetry*, *Wheels* included the work of Trench Poets. It had the honour of being the first collection to recognise the genius of Wilfred Owen, seven of whose poems were included in the Fourth Cycle, which is dedicated to his memory. The main achieve-ment of *Wheels*, however, was to offer an alternative to the tame naturalism and vague romanticism of the Georgians. This alternative is to be found chiefly in the contributions of the three Sitwells, and especially those of Edith Sitwell. These contributions consist of a kind of 'non-representational' poetry with strong affinities to the 'non-representational' art of contemporary painters such as the Cubists and Picasso. It is worth noting that the cover of the First Cycle of *Wheels* is decorated with a perfectly traditional satiric drawing, while the cover designs of later Cycles are highly 'modern-istic' works by Laurence Atkinson and others.

In her early poetry Edith Sitwell uses fancy more seriously and more successfully than any English poet since the seventeenth century. Like the best pastoral poets of that period such as Marvell she creates a fanciful world with a peculiar imaginative intensity and her fancy has a highly sensuous quality. 'My senses', she wrote, 'are like those of primitive people, at once acute and uncovered—and they are interchangeable!' This 'interchange of the senses' gives her imagery an unusual power and produces that richness of 'texture' which she prizes so highly:—

> The farm-pond, fruitish-soft and ripe,
> Was smooth as a daguerrotype;
>
> The farm-maid, Rosa, under flimsy
> Muslin skies, an angel's whimsy,

> Walked . . . Her daisy-frilléd frock
> Was stiff and harder than a rock.

The world of these early poems of Edith Sitwell is derived from fairy tales, the Russian ballet and personal memories. It is a world of rich and varied beauty full of symbolic figures, Gargotte, the goosegirl, the good fairy Chatte Blanche and the bad fairy Laidronette, the princess and the governess, Mrs Troy the house-keeper, Zambo the negro boy and many others. Some of these poems come very close to that *poésie pure* which was the dream of certain Continental theorists. It is a poetry of pure sensuous ecstasy, like some of the early poems of the Pre-Raphaelites:—

> The kingly cock with his red-gold beard,
> And his red-gold crown had crowed unheard
>
> While his queens ruffled down
> Their feathered gown
> Beside the waterfall's crystal town;
>
> The cock, the dawn-fruits, the gold corn,
> Sing this aubade, cold, forlorn.

Edith Sitwell was, however, too great a poet to remain for long in this paradise of sensuous imagination. Her tenderness and humanity were already finding expression in such poems as 'The Man with the Green Patch' and 'Colonel Fantock' or the lovely lines on youth in 'The Sleeping Beauty':

> When we were young, how beautiful life seemed!—
> The boundless bright horizons that we dreamed,
>
> And the immortal music of the Day and Night,
> Leaving the echo of their wonder and their might
>
> Deep in our hearts and minds. How could the dust
> Of superstitions taught in schoolrooms, lust
>
> In love's shape, dim our beauty? What dark lie,
> Or cruelty's voice, could drown this God-made harmony?

'Cruelty's voice', the vision of the horror of the contemporary world breaks in more and more on the crystalline beauty of her earlier poetry and is symbolised by such figures as Sir Pompey

Alexander, the rich, stupid philistine, Dr Gradus, the solumn, dry pedant, and Mrs Behemoth, the possessive female. The lyric sweetness of her poetry is touched with satire and irony when these figures appear, and there is a rising strain of indignation against the stupidity and cruelty of the contemporary world, reaching a terrifying culmination in the poem called *Gold Coast Customs* (1929). Here the world of the cannibal West African negroes, as described by Hegel, with its complete but unselfconscious inhumanity, is used as an image of the far worse hypocritical humanity of a society consisting of heartless possessors of wealth like the inane Lady Bamburgher and their inevitable accompaniment, the sordid horror of the slums:

> I have seen the murdered God look through the eyes
> Of the drunkard's smirched
> Mask as he lurched
> O'er the half of my heart that lies in the street
> 'Neath the dancing fleas and the foul news-sheet.
> Where (a black gap flapping,
> A white skin drum)
> The cannibal houses
> Watch this come—
> Lady Bamburgher's party; for the plan
> Is a prize for those that on all fours ran
> Through the rotting slum
> Till those who come
> Could never guess from the mud-covered shapes
> Which are the rich or the mired dire apes,
> As they run where the souls, dirty paper, are blown
> In the hour before dawn, through this long hell of stone.

Gold Coast Customs is a great prophetic work, a tragic vision of the contemporary world comparable with *The Waste Land* and *Sweeney Agonistes*. But it is not a poem of despair. Its appalling horror is combined with a faith in a divine cleansing power that will ultimately triumph:

> When the rich man's gold and the rich man's wheat
> Will grow in the street, that the starved may eat,—
> And the sea of the rich will give up its dead—

II

Early in the second half of the inter-war period, a new group of young poets began to attract attention. They had been friends at Oxford where they were undergraduates in 1927-9. The group was dominated by the powerful personality of Wystan Hugh Auden (1907-   ), the son of a Yorkshire doctor, who was interested both in psychology and in literature. Auden became a legendary figure while he was still at Oxford. He studied biology as well as literature and insisted that poetry should be 'clinical'. Of the many stories about the young Auden the most significant is perhaps that told by his tutor Neville Coghill:

> One morning Mr Wystan Auden, then an undergraduate at Christ Church blew in to Exeter College for his tutorial with me saying, 'I have torn up all my poems'. 'Indeed! Why?' 'Because they are no good. Based on Wordsworth. No good nowadays.' 'Oh. . . . ?' 'You ought to read Eliot. I've been reading Eliot. I now see the way I want to write. . . .'[1]

After leaving Oxford, Auden spent some years in Germany and then worked as a schoolmaster. Both these experiences had important effects on his poetry. The other members of the group were Cecil Day Lewis (1904-   ), the son of an Irish clergyman. Stephen Spender (1909-   ), a youth of Anglo-Jewish descent from a London suburban home, and Louis MacNeice (1907-1963), an Ulsterman and a brilliant classical scholar. The whole of this New Country group,[2] as they have been called, reacted strongly against the doctrine of 'art for art's sake' and what they called 'luxury poetry'. They would all have subscribed to MacNeice's view that 'a poet should be able-bodied, fond of talking, a reader of the newspapers, capable of pity and laughter, informed in economics, appreciative of women, involved in personal relationships, actively interested in politics, susceptible to physical impressions'. Day Lewis in his critical essay 'A Hope for Poetry' (1933) claimed G. M. Hopkins, Owen and Eliot as the 'immediate ancestors' of the group and they were also considerably influenced by D. H. Lawrence and the later poetry of Yeats. They were much less bookish than Eliot and were far more interested than he was in the contemporary political situation. Indeed their work can be described as a new attempt to make the 'voyage without' while

[1] *A Symposium on T. S. Eliot*, Ed. March and Tambimuttu (1949), p. 82.
[2] Their works were introduced to the public in *New Signatures* (1932) and *New Country* (1933).

retaining the gains of the 'voyage within' which has been achieved
by such explorers as Eliot and Lawrence. They suffered, however,
from handicaps which were unknown to such earlier 'outward
voyagers' as Kipling and Chesterton. Serious writers were now
separated by an ever widening gulf from the mass of the reading
public, a division which was well expressed by the adoption at
about this time of the American terms 'highbrow' and 'lowbrow'.
The contact of Kipling with a world of soldiers, sailors and barmaids
who knew countless popular tunes and music hall songs was now
as impossible as Chesterton's connection with a living middle class
poetic culture. The 'New Country' poets used slang, jazzy metres
and imagery derived from machinery and boys' stories but their
technique of expression was the Symbolist idiom learnt from Eliot,
which was quite incomprehensible to the lowbrow. Their politics
were Marxian, and they sought to combine Karl Marx's philosophy
of revolution with Freud's psychology of the unconscious. To
achieve such a synthesis was, perhaps, beyond their power, and in
any case, as Day Lewis has pointed out in *The Poetic Image* (1947),
the ideals of Marx and Freud were not generally accepted and the
result was a certain hollowness and emotional thinness in their
poetry, which often gives the impression of being written in a sort
of private family language and of being addressed rather self-
consciously and exclusively to the initiated. Nevertheless, Auden
and his friends brought back into poetry a new virility and a new
sense of the contemporary situation in England. Moreover, their
left wing politics are the expression of 'a fine virtue of social
generosity and human sympathy, an inner radiance of thought and
feeling', qualities that had been rare in English poetry since the days
of Byron and Shelley.

The Spanish Civil War and the rise of the Nazi-Fascist terror in
Europe gave the New Country poets for a few years a heroic
myth which moved them as deeply as the European democratic
movement of the eighteen-twenties moved Byron, Shelley and
Leigh Hunt. Auden's *The Orators* (1930) is as incoherent, and as
full of private jokes and undergraduate humour as his *Poems* of
1929. The volume, however, concludes with six Odes which have
a strength and a controlled passion beyond anything which Auden
had hitherto written. This new power was developed in the magnificent lyrical realism of the poems in *Look Stranger* (1936), and the
noble energy of 'Spain' (1937).

Day Lewis celebrated the heroic exploit of a Spanish government
trawler in 'The Nabara', a spirited attempt to revive the narrative

ballad, and in 'The Volunteer', an epitaph on the Englishmen who
fell fighting with the International Brigade, achieved a classic
lucidity and directness unparalleled in the work of the New
Country poets:

> Tell them in England, if they ask
> What brought us to these wars,
> To this plateau beneath the night's
> Grave manifold of stars—
>
> It was not fraud or foolishness,
> Glory, revenge or pay:
> We came because our open eyes
> Could see no other way.

Auden's *Poems* of 1930 contains much that is incoherent, much
private jargon, and a certain amount of priggishness. He draws
his imagery not from history and mythology, but from the school
changing room and playing field as well as from the modern street
and industrial scene, and also from the boys' magazine and adventure
story. At times he speaks like a public school master who has
emancipated himself from the old public school prejudices and has
read Freud and Marx, but still retains the public school admiration
for toughness and the team spirit. His advice, as conveyed in the
famous prayer that concludes the volume, is excellent, but, to use Day-
Lewis's expression, its expression had a certain 'emotional thinness':

> Prohibit sharply the rehearsed response
> And gradually correct the coward's stance;
> Cover in time with beams those in retreat
> That, spotted, they turn though the reverse were great,
> Publish each healer that in city lives
> Or country houses at the end of drives;
> Harrow the house of the dead; look shining at
> New styles of architecture, a change of heart.

This 'emotional thinness' is corrected in certain poems by a notable
lyrical gift and also by Auden's passionate apprehension of the
English scene, as in the fine poem in the metre of 'Locksley Hall'
on the England of the great slump, which has a vigour and raciness
recalling the best of Kipling:

> Get there if you can and see the land you once were proud to own
> Though the roads have almost vanished and the expresses never run:

G

Smokeless chimneys, damaged bridges, rotting wharves and choked canals,
Tramlines buckled, smashed trucks lying on their sides across the rails;

Power-stations locked, deserted, since they drew the boiler fires;
Pylons falling or subsiding, trailing dead high-tension wires; . . .
. . . .
Where the Sunday lads come talking motor bicycle and girl,
Smoking cigarettes in chains until their heads are in a whirl.

Far from there we spent the money, thinking we could well afford,
While they quietly undersold us with their cheaper trade abroad.

Day Lewis, a slightly older man than Auden, published his
Transitional Poem in 1929, a sequence with erudite notes in the
manner which Eliot had made fashionable in the nineteen-twenties.
Both this work and its two successors *From Feathers to Iron* (1931)
and *The Magnetic Mountain* (1933) show signs of the influence of
Auden, who is quoted and sometimes directly addressed. Sometimes Day Lewis writes lines that might be mistaken for the work
of Auden in his gusty satiric mood:

Smile! All together! You'll soon be better,
Have you a grouch? Do you feel an itch?
There, there! Sit down and write uncle a letter,
Lock the front door, here are your slippers,
Get out your toys and don't make a noise,
Don't tease the keepers, eat up your kippers,
And you'll have a treat one day if you're good boys.

But Day Lewis's characteristic work is to be found less in this
breezy sort of satire than in the lyrics which have a quietness, a
clarity and a sweetness rarely found in the English poetry of his
time:

Now she is like the white tree-rose
That takes a blessing from the sun:
Summer has filled her veins with light,
And her warm heart is washed with noon.

Or as a poplar, ceaselessly
Gives a soft answer to the wind:
Cool on the light her leaves lie sleeping,
Folding a column of sweet sound.

Like Auden he has a strong sense of the English scene and a power
of presenting it with a flowing music which is quite unlike Auden's
harsh, arresting discords:

> You that love England, who have an ear for her music,
> The slow movement of clouds in benediction,
> Clear arias of light thrilling over her uplands,
> Over the chords of summer sustained peacefully;
> Ceaseless the leaves counterpoint in a west wind lively,
> Blossom and river rippling loveliest allegro,
> And the storms of wood strings brass at year's finale:
> Listen. Can you not hear the entrance of a new theme?

Stephen Spender and Louis MacNeice, the two younger members of the 'New Country Group' had little in common beyond the fact that they had the same 'poetic ancestry' and both felt the liberating influence of Auden. Spender was the most introspective and MacNeice the most objective and 'hardboiled'. Although he adopted the fashionable Marxism of the 'thirties, Spender has always been a liberal romantic in the tradition of Shelley. The Communist myth, which for Auden was a sort of glorified public school with a touch of the *Kameradschaft* of the German youth movement and for Day Lewis simply the English countryside freed from commercialism and snobbery, for Spender was a liberation of the individual spirit like that prophesied by Shelley in *Promethus Unbound*:—

> Not palaces, an era's crown
> Where the mind dwells, intrigues, rests;
> The architectural gold-leafed flower
> From people ordered like a single mind,
> I build. This only what I tell:
> It is too late for rare accumulation
> For family pride, for beauty's filtered dusts;
> I say, stamping the words with emphasis,
> Drink from here energy, and only energy,
> As from the electric charge of a battery. . . .
> . . . .
> No spirit seek here rest. But this: No man
> Shall hunger; Man shall spend equally.
> Our goal which we compel: Man shall be man.

Alone among the New Country poets MacNeice failed to respond to the myth of the Communist State. He was a keen and pitiless critic of contemporary England with no vision of a Utopian future, and was extremely successful in making poetry out of the modern urban scene:

Smoke from the train-gulf hid by hoardings blunders upward, the
  brakes of cars
Pipe as the policeman pivoting round, raises his flat hand, bars
With his figure of a monolith Pharaoh the queue of fidgety machines
(Chromium dogs on the bonnet, faces behind the triplex screens),
Behind him the streets run away between the proud glass of shops,
Cubical scent-bottles, artificial legs, arctic foxes and electric mops.

MacNeice is seen at his best as an objective, realistic painter in
verse. His attempts at philosophising lack emotional depth and
tend to become cleverly versified prose, but he has great metrical
accomplishment and a bitter Irish humour which finds notable
expression in such poems as the delightful 'Bagpipe Music'.

Auden made a series of experiments in poetic drama in the
nineteen-thirties. The earliest of these was *The Dog Beneath the
Skin* (1935), a political and moral fable in the form of an expres-
sionist revue, or musical comedy. The most successful parts of it
are the choruses with their magnificent sweeping views of contemporary English landscape. In *The Ascent of F6* (1936), written in
collaboration with Christopher Isherwood, Auden uses a similar
technique to dramatise a story of adventure probably suggested by
the career of T. E. Lawrence and also related to the boys' stories
which form the background of much of his early poetry. Although
it contains passages of great poetic power the play lacks unity and
coherence. Political and social satire are jumbled with Freudian
psychology and an unexpected vein of sentimentality. *On the
Frontier* (1938), also by Auden and Isherwood is a stronger and
better integrated play, a kind of dramatised poster or cartoon
satirising with crude power the nationalist and fascist movements
of contemporary Europe. The most successful attempt, however,
at a political morality play symbolising the European crises in the
years immediately preceding the Second World War was Stephen
Spender's *Trial of a Judge* (1938). This poem has a unity as well as a
subtlety of thought and feeling which Auden and Isherwood with
all their brilliance never achieved. Although it arises from the
contemporary situation, it is a parable which has a permanent
value. The judge is the spirit of European liberalism. His refusal
to condone the crimes committed in the name of nationalism, his
trial and condemnation are a symbol of tragedies which were being
enacted all over Europe in 1938 and 1939 but his argument with the
red prisioners in gaol is a memorable affirmation of principles that
lie at the very centre of the tradition of European humanism:

> if we use their methods
> Of lies and hate, then we betray
> The achievement in ourselves; our truth
> Becomes the prisoner of necessity
> Equally with their untruth. . . .

The New Country movement ended with the outbreak of the Second World War. The signing of the Russo-German Pact in the summer of 1939 destroyed the myth of the Communist State as the defender of European liberty, which had been the centre of their doctrine. On the eve of the outbreak of war Auden crossed the Atlantic and became an American citizen. The group had performed notable services to English poetry. They widened the range of its rhythm and imagery, gave it a new and healthy worldliness and brought it into close touch with English and the European political scenes. Their success was only limited. Their 'outward voyage' was a failure because, in spite of desperate efforts, they failed to establish contact with any large group of their fellow countrymen and remained to the end a coterie of brilliant intellectuals. Julian Bell (1908–1937), a young poet of great promise, who was killed while driving a lorry for the Spanish Republicans, pointed out their weaknesses with great critical insight in his 'Open Letter to Day Lewis',[1] where he condemns their 'enormous painting of fancy pictures of the future Socialist State', their '*simpliste* applications of the red and white morality' ('Auden's nice young Scouts are always so nice'), and their 'private language, esoteric jokes, fantasies and whims'. Nevertheless, although they failed to provide modern England with a truly popular poetry, their movement had a great value in stimulating the genius of four considerable poets. Of these Day Lewis has shown, perhaps, the most interesting and hopeful development. As his reply to Julian Bell shows,[2] he was quite aware, at an early date, of the weaknesses of the Auden group. His own later poetry has moved away from the 'crude over-simplification' and the 'private language' of the original New Country poetry towards a balanced and humane art which connects him with the tradition of Thomas Hardy rather than with that of Auden and his 'ancestors'.

---

[1] Julian Bell, *Essays, Poems, Letters* (1938), pp. 306-328.
[2] Ibid, pp. 328-334.

III

In the 'Postscript' written in 1936, appended to the second edition
of *A Hope for Poetry*, Day Lewis noted 'the appearance of a new
generation of poets not so much influenced by the New Country
school as reacting away from it'. It is, perhaps, a measure of the
partial failure or limited success of that school that the most
promising of their younger contemporaries were not impelled to
continue that 'voyage without' which Auden and his friends had
initiated with such a flourish of trumpets, but rather felt the need
of a fresh exploration of the inner life, or, in the words of Day Lewis,
'a return to the ideals of poetic integrity and artistic individualism:
a setting-out-again in the direction of "pure" poetry'. In the limited
space available here it is only possible to give a very brief indication
of the products of this 'new romanticism' of the late 'thirties and
early 'forties. The chief names associated with it are those of
George Barker (1913–   ), David Gascoyne (1916–   ) and
Dylan Thomas (1914–1953). They all probably owe a considerable
debt to Edith Sitwell and they were also influenced by the Surrealist
movement, which had begun in France in the nineteen-twenties
and which received a good deal of publicity in England when the
first International Surrealist Exhibition was held in London in
June, 1936. Surrealism, like its predecessor Dada (the invention of
the Rumanian Tristan Tzara), with which it had close connections,
was a theory of 'pure' art, 'a reaffirmation', as Herbert Read, one
of its chief English exponents, wrote, 'of the romantic principle'.
Surrealism was essentially anti-rational. Its essential basis was said
by Georges Hugnet to be 'automatism' and one of its chief aims
was to 'lift writing to the plane of exaltation'. The surrealists
declared themselves to be dialectical materialists and enemies of the
capitalist state, but they were entirely opposed to 'socialist realism',
the official doctrine of art in the u.s.s.r., and the Communists did
not welcome them as allies. Their theories naturally found a good
deal of support in the country of Blake, Coleridge and Lewis Carroll.
    George Barker in his *Thirty Preliminary Poems* (1933), *Poems*
(1935), *Calamiterror* (1937), and *Lament and Triumph* (1940) showed
himself as a poet with a strong visionary imagination and a power
of creating flowing rhythms of great beauty. There is much that
is confused and obscure in these poems, a welter of imagery,
which occasionally clarifies in passages and whole poems
of pure lyrical quality like the 'Allegory of the Adolescent and the
Adult':

It was when weather was Arabian I went
Over the downs to Alton where winds were wounded
With flowers and swathed me with aroma, I walked
Like Saint Christopher Columbus through a sea's welter
Of gaudy ways looking for a wonder.

Although he wrote some moving poetry on the Spanish Civil War, Barker's chief subject is the exploration of the inner life. He rarely uses ironical clichés like the New Country poets, but looks at life with a rapt vision like that of Blake or De la Mare:

With burning fervour
I am forever
Turning in my hand
The crystal, this moment.

David Gascoyne was strongly influenced for a time by the theories of the Surrealists. He has much in common with Barker: a power of dream-like vision and a profusion of obscure, violent and sometimes powerful imagery. His most memorable work was done when he abandoned strict adherence to surrealist doctrine and expressed with great delicacy and power the impact of the misery of wartime England on a sensitive spirit:

Draw now with pricking hand the curtains back;
Unpin the black-out cloth; let in
Grim crack-of-dawn's first glimmer through the glass.
All's yet half sunk in Yesterday's stale death,
Obscurely still beneath a moist-tinged blank
Sky like the inside of a deaf mute's mouth.

Of all the younger poets of the nineteen-thirties Dylan Thomas had the most brilliant lyrical gift. This young Welshman in his *Eighteen Poems* (1934) and *Twenty Five Poems* (1936) used language with an originality and a daring felicity that had hardly been paralleled since Hopkins. His poetry, like that of Barker and Gascoyne, is full of violent images of death, and love. As Edwin Muir has pointed out, it has 'to a high degree the "natural magic" which Arnold attributed to the Celtic genius'. *The Map of Love* (1939), his third volume, is a mixed collection of prose and verse. Among much that is confused and obscure, it contains poetry of great strength and a deeper humanity than any of the work of the 'new romantics'—as in the noble elegy on the old Welsh servant Ann Jones:

But I, Ann's bard on a raised hearth, call all
The seas to service that her wood-tongued virtue
Babble like a bellbuoy over the hymning heads,
Bow down the walls of the ferned and foxy woods
That her love sing and swing through a brown chapel,
Bless her bent spirit with four, crossing birds.
Her flesh was meek as milk, but this skyward statue
With the wild breast and blessed and giant skull
Is carved from her in a room with a wet window
In a fiercely mourning house in a crooked year.

The most important development in English poetry at the time
of the beginning of the Second World War, was, however, the
full flowering of the genius of Edith Sitwell. After the publication
of *Gold Coast Customs*, she wrote no poetry for several years. The
emotional shock caused by the vivid apprehension of the ugliness
and cruelty of the modern world which produced the terrifying
effect of *Gold Coast Customs*, seems in some way to have been
absorbed and transmuted by her study of the character of Swift
in her novel, *I Live Under a Black Sun* (1936), and also by her
extensive reading of the works of some of the great religious
mystics and of ancient Greek poetry. In the first years of the war,
she produced a wonderfully rich and splendid harvest of poetry
which was collected in *Street Songs* (1942) and *Green Song* (1944).
This new poetry of Edith Sitwell was among the notable achievements of European literature in the twentieth century. It had all
the fresh brilliance and clear music of her earlier work, combined
with a much deeper philosophical outlook and a keener apprehension of the tragedy of humanity in the twentieth century. Now
she had not only apprehended this tragedy, but she had transcended
it by a new consciousness of the unity of being:

For the sun is the first lover of the world,
Blessing all humble creatures, all life-giving,
Blessing the end of life and the work done,
The clean and the unclean, ores in earth, and splendours
Within the heart of man, that second sun.

Here there is a true integration of the inner and outer worlds, a
healing of the 'schism in the soul' similar to that achieved by
Yeats in his later poems and Eliot in the *Four Quartets*. In 'Still Falls
the Rain', the great poem on the Air Raids of 1940, the tragic
vision of *Gold Coast Customs* is combined with a kind of heroic
faith in divine love:

Still falls the Rain—
Still falls the Blood from the Starved Man's wounded Side:
He bears in His Heart all wounds,—those of the light that died,
The last faint spark
In the self-murdered heart, the wounds of the sad uncomprehending dark,
The wounds of the baited bear,—
The blind and weeping bear whom the keepers beat
On his helpless flesh . . . the tears of the hunted hare.

Still falls the Rain—
Then—O Ile leape up to my God: who pulles me doune—
See, see where Christ's blood streames in the firmament:
It flows from the Brow we nailed upon the tree
Deep to the dying, to the thirsting heart
That holds the fires of the world,—dark-smirched with pain
As Caesar's laurel crown.

Then sounds the voice of One who like the heart of man
Was once a child who among beasts has lain—
'Still do I love, still shed my innocent light, my Blood, for thee'.

What is specially remarkable in this poem is the author's power of investing ancient symbols with new meaning. Her crucified Christ in this poem is no mere pious allegory but the living embodiment of the suffering of the whole world (including the animals) identified in a flash of inspired imagination with the incarnation of divine love. The style of Edith Sitwell in these later poems is an astonishing feat. Her years of experiment culminated in a technique which combined the freedom of *vers libre* with the sweetness and harmony of the old rhyming metres, and a richness of texture unequalled since Hopkins. Much of this poetry is naturally occupied with a tragic vision of a world at war, but this vision is irradiated by a constructive faith, a vivid apprehension of the divine nature of the world. This faith is not tied to any dogmatic orthodoxy but is a kind of Christian pantheism reviving and continuing the great English tradition of Spenser, Milton, Blake and Wordsworth, and showing the universe not as dead matter but as the true manifestation of God which men can reach not merely with intellect but with the senses:

The flame of the first blade
Is an angel piercing through the earth to sing
'God is everything!
The grass within the grass, the angel in the angel, flame

Within the flame, and He is the green shade that came
To be the heart of shade'.

. . . .

He is the sea of ripeness and the sweet apple's emerald lore.
So you, my flame of grass, my root of the world from which all
      Spring shall grow,
O you, my hawthorn bough of the stars, now leaning low
Through the day, for your flowers to kiss my lips, shall know
He is the core of the heart of love, and He, beyond labouring seas,
      an ultimate shore.

Although it lies outside the strict chronological limit of this study,
and although it deserves very much fuller treatment than that
which can be given to it here, it may be fitting to end this survey
with a reference to Edith Sitwell's great philosophic poem *The
Shadow of Cain* (1946). This poem is a prophetic vision of the
modern crisis and a revelation of its significance. It shows humanity
emerging from the 'Ancient Cold' of the Glacial Age and splitting
into the duality of rich and poor symbolised by the tiger and the
bird. This spiritual cleavage culminates in, and is symbolised by,
the explosion of the atom bomb at Hiroshima when

                    the Primal Matter
      Was broken, the womb from which all life began, . . .

In the hollow of the split atom lie the two men, who are the two
halves of Man, Lazarus and Dives, each with his symbol of gold—
gold as the life-giving wheat and gold as money, which is death
and corruption. There is a kind of apocalyptic dialogue between
the two men and the two golds, Lazarus who is mistaken for
Christ in the new age, and Dives who thinks his gold can cure all
the ills of the world. Out of that dialogue, the modern crisis faced
and understood, will arise a new unity, 'Christ the whole man'.

      Think! When the last clamour of the Bought and Sold
      The agony of Gold
      Is hushed. . . . When the last Judas-kiss
      Has died upon the Cheek of the Starved Man Christ, those ashes
            that were men
      Will rise again
      To be our Fires upon the Judgment Day!
      And yet—who dreamed that Christ has died in vain?
      He walks again on the Seas of Blood, He comes in the terrible Rain.

The great achievement of English poetry in the period surveyed in this study is that it has remained alive in a world which has become increasingly hostile to all the values for which the poet stands. In the fourth decade of the twentieth century it was, indeed, heartening to see it represented by the work of such artists as T. S. Eliot, Edith Sitwell and C. Day Lewis and to find that it was the chief preoccupation of some of the finest spirits who died in the war against Nazi tyranny, such as Sidney Keyes and Alun Lewis. In a sense it might be said that English poetry had by this time overcome its 'internal crisis', the cleavage between the modernists and the traditionalists. The mature poetry of Eliot, Edith Sitwell or Day Lewis cannot be called 'modernist' or 'traditionalist'. It has absorbed the lessens of 'modernism' and combined them with those elements of the English tradition which can live in the modern world. It is the 'external crisis' of English poetry that remains unsolved. In order to maintain its integrity it has been forced to restrict its appeal to a small part of the population. F. R. Leavis has written that 'without a public poetry can hardly survive and the ordinary cultivated reader is ceasing to read poetry at all'. This is an important truth. Poetry must indeed continue to look inward, but it must also look outward, and regain contact with a wider audience. 'Probably', writes Day Lewis, 'poetry can never be popular again in the degree that the cinema is popular at the moment', but it could reach a very much wider section of the 'ordinary cultivated' public than it does at present. Through them it could play an important part in humanising the classless (and at present cultureless) society of the Welfare State by providing it with living images of virtue and truth, which would help to heal 'the schism in the soul' caused by standardisation and mechanisation, and ultimately to restore that 'whole man' whose resurrection is prophesied by Edith Sitwell in the majestic parable of *The Shadow of Cain*.

BIBLIOGRAPHY

INTRODUCTION

SPENSER, Edmund: Letter to Sir Walter Ralegh appended to *The Faerie Queene*

ARNOLD, Matthew: 'The Study of Poetry' in *Essays in Criticism* (second series)

TENNYSON, Alfred, Lord: *The Princess* (1847)

GISSING, George: *Demos* (1886)

TREVELYAN, G. M.: *English Social History*

TOYNBEE, Arnold: *A Study of History* (abridgment by D. C. Somervell)

CHAPTER I

MASTERMAN, C. F. G.: *The Condition of England*, Ed. with introduction by J. T. Boulton (1960)

CAPETANAKIS, Demetrios: *A Greek Poet in England* (1947)

MEREDITH, George: *Celt and Saxon* (1910)

VERLAINE, Paul: *Poèmes Saturniens*

WILDE, Oscar: *Collected Works*

YEATS, W. B.: *Autobiographies*

DOWSON, Ernest: *Poems*, Ed. D. Flower (1934)

JOHNSON, Lionel: *Poetical Works* (1926)
   Postliminium (Critical Essays)

SHORTHOUSE, J. H.: *John Inglesant* (1881)

SYMONS, Arthur: *The Symbolist Movement in Literature* (1889)
   Aubrey Beardsley (1898)
   Poems (2 vols. 1924)

BURDETT, Osbert: *The Beardsley Period*

SYMONS, A. J. A.: *An Anthology of 'Nineties' Verse*

TILLOTSON, G.: *Essays in Criticism and Research* (1942)

BLUNT, W. S.: *Collected Poems* (2 vols. 1914)

The Poetry of Wilfred Scawen Blunt, selected and arranged by W. E. Henley
  and George Wyndham (1898)
FINCH, Edith: *Wilfred Scawen Blunt 1840–1922* (1938)
BLUNT, W. S.: *My Diaries 1888–1914*
HENLEY, W. E.: *Collected Works*
BUCKLEY, J. H.: *William Ernest Henley* (Princeton, 1948)
SIMS, G. R.: *Ballads and Poems* (1883)
KIPLING, Rudyard: *Collected Verse*
     Kim
     A Little of Myself
A Choice of Kipling's Verse, Ed. T. S. Eliot (1941)
CARRINGTON, C. E.: *Rudyard Kipling, his Life and Work* (1955)
Kipling's Mind and Art, Ed. A. Rutherford (1964). (Contains the important
  essays by G. Orwell, E. Wilson and L. Trilling)
DAVIDSON, John: *Poems and Ballads* selected with an introduction by
  R. D. Macleod (1959)
     (For complete list of Davidson's works, and an acute criticism of his poetry
     see B. Ifor Evans, *English Poetry in the later Nineteenth Century*)

                              CHAPTER 2

HARDY, Thomas: *Wessex Novels*
     Collected Poems
     The Dynasts
HARDY, Florence: *The Life of Thomas Hardy* (2 vols, 1933)
JOHNSON, Lionel: *Thomas Hardy* (new ed. with chapter on the poetry by
  A. E. Barton, 1923)
ABERCROMBIE, Lascelles: *Thomas Hardy* (1919)
RUTLAND, W. R.: *Thomas Hardy* (1938)
CHAKRAVARTY, A.: *The Dynasts and the Post-War Age in Poetry* (1938)
BOWRA, C. M.: *The Lyrical Poetry of Thomas Hardy* (Byron Foundation
  Lecture, Nottingham, 1946)
HOUSMAN, A. E.: *Collected Poems* (1953), Penguin edn., 1956
HOUSMAN, Laurence: *A.E.H.* (1937)
RICHARDS, Grant: *Housman 1897–1936* (1941)

                              CHAPTER 3

WHITMAN, Walt: *Complete Poetry and Selected Prose and Letters*, Ed.
  E. Holloway
MASTERS, Edgar Lee: *Whitman* (New York, 1937)
SANTAYANA, G.: *Interpretations of Poetry and Religion* (1900)
     Winds of Doctrine (1913)
HOPKINS, Gerard Manley: *Poems*, Ed. Bridges (1918)
     Poems (Ed. W. H. Gardner, 1956)
     Letters to Robert Bridges (Ed. C. C. Abbott)
     The Correspondence of Gerard Manley Hopkins and R. W. Dixon (Ed.
       C. C. Abbott)
     The Notebooks and Papers of Gerard Manley Hopkins (Ed. Humphry
       House)
     Further Letters of Gerard Manley Hopkins (Ed. C. C. Abbott)

GARDNER, W. H.: *Gerard Manley Hopkins* (2 vols., 1944–1949)
BRIDGES, Robert: *Poetical Works* (1936)
    The Testament of Beauty (1930)
    Collected Essays, Papers (1927–36)
    Poetry and Prose, Ed. Sparrow (1935)
    Three Friends (1932)
THOMPSON, Edward: *Robert Bridges* (1944)
RITZ, J. G.: *Robert Bridges and Gerard Hopkins, 1863–1889: a Literary Friendship* (1960)
YEATS, W. B.: *The Oxford Book of Modern Verse* (Introduction)

CHAPTER 4

YEATS, William Butler: *Collected Poems*
    Collected Plays
    Autobiographies
    Mythologies
    The Letters of W. B. Yeats
    The Variorum Edition of the Poems of W. B. Yeats, Ed. P. Allt and R. K. Alspach (New York, 1957)
HONE, Joseph: *W. B. Yeats 1865–1939* (1942)
JEFFARES, A. N.: *W. B. Yeats, Man and Poet* (1949)
    'The Byzantine Poems of W. B. Yeats' (*Review of English Studies*, XXII, 1946, p. 44)
MENON, V. K. Narayana: *The Development of W. B. Yeats* (1942)
HOARE, Dorothy: *The Works of Morris and Yeats in Relation to Early Saga Literature* (1937)
URE, P.: *Towards a Mythology, Studies in the Poetry of W. B. Yeats* (1946)
ELLMANN, R.: *The Identity of Yeats* (1957)
WILSON, F. A. C.: *W. B. Yeats and Tradition* (1958)
Essays on Yeats by C. M. Bowra in *The Heritage of Symbolism*, E. Wilson in *Axel's Castle*, Stephen Spender in *The Destructive Element*, and L. C. Knights in *Explorations*
SYNGE, J. M.: *Collected Works*, Ed. Skelton (1963–6)
GREENE, D. H. and STEPHENS, E. M.: *J. M. Synge, 1871–1900* (1959)
HOWARTH, H.: *The Irish Writers* (1958)
The Oxford Book of Irish Verse, Ed. MacDonagh and Lennox Robinson (1958)

CHAPTER 5

MASTERMAN, C. F. G.: op. cit.
SINCLAIR, May: *The Divine Fire* (1904)
JAMES, Henry: *The Wings of a Dove* (1902)
    The Ambassadors (1903)
    The Golden Bowl (1905)
FORSTER, E. M.: *The Longest Journey* (1907)
HOBHOUSE, L. T.: *Democracy and Reaction* (1909)
WATSON, Sir William: *Collected Poems*, 2 vols (1906)

CHESTERTON, G. K.: *The Napoleon of Notting Hill* (1904)
  The Man Who Was Thursday (1908)
  The Flying Inn (1914)
  The Wild Knight (1900)
  The Ballad of the White Horse (1911)
  Poems (1915)
  Wine, Water and Song (1915)
  Collected Poems (1927)
DE LA MARE, Walter: *Songs of Childhood* (1902)
  Poems (1906)
  The Listeners and Other Poems (1912)
  Motley and Other Poems (1918)
  The Veil and Other Poems (1921)
  Pleasures and Speculations (Critical Essays) (1940)
  Collected Poems, 2 vols. (1942)
REID, Forrest: *Walter de la Mare, a Critical Study* (1929)
ABERCROMBIE, Lascelles: *Poems* (1930)
  The Sale of St Thomas in Six Acts (1930)
MASEFIELD, John: *Collected Poems*
DAVIES, W. H.: *Collected Poems*
Georgian Poetry—1911–12, 1913–15, 1916–17, 1918–19 and 1920–22
MARSH, Sir Edward: *A Number of People* (1939)
Articles on 'Georgian Poetry' by B. Rajan in *The Critic*, Autumn, 1948, and
  on 'The Georgian Poets' by A. Pryce Jones in Penguin *New Writing*,
  No. 35, (1947)
THOMAS, Edward: *Collected Poems*, Preface by Walter de la Mare (1920)
MOORE, John: *The Life and Letters of Edward Thomas* (1939)
HUXLEY, Aldous: 'Edward Thomas' in *On the Margin*
BLUNDEN, Edmund: *Poems 1914–30* (1930)
  An Elegy and Other Poems (1937)
  Shells by a Stream (1945)
  Poems of Many Years, Ed. Hart Davis (1957)

CHAPTER 6

JOHNSTON, J. H.: *English Poetry of the First World War* (1964)
BERGONZI, B.: *Heroes' Twilight* (1965)
BROOKE, Rupert: *Collected Poems*
  Letters from America
HASSALL, C.: *Rupert Brooke, a Biography* (1964)
Soldier Poets, Ed. Galloway Kyle (1916)
An Anthology of War Poems, Ed. F. Brereton (Introduction by E. C. Blunden,
  1930)
SITWELL, Sir Osbert: *Left Hand Right Hand: An Autobiography* (1945–50)
BLUNDEN, Edmund: *Undertones of War* (1928)
SORLEY, C. H.: *Marlborough and Other Poems* (4th, enlarged ed., 1919)
  The Letters of Charles Sorley (1919)
PRESS, John: 'Charles Sorley' *A Review of English Literature*, VII, 2 April
  1966

SASSOON, Siegfried: *The Daffodil Murderer* (1913)
 The Old Huntsman (1917)
 Counter-Attack (1918)
 Collected Poems (1947)
 Memoirs of a Foxhunting Man (1928)
 Memoirs of An Infantry Officer (1930)
 Sherston's Progress (1936)
 The Old Century (1938)
 The Weald of Youth (1942)
 Siegfried's Journey (1945)
THORPE, M.: *Siegfried Sassoon* (1966)
GRAVES, Robert: *Over the Brazier* (1916)
 Fairies and Fusiliers (1917)
 Goodbye to All That (1929)
 Collected Poems (1938)
OWEN, Wilfred: *Poems* (with an Introduction by Siegfried Sassoon) (1920)
 Poems (Ed. E. Blunden) (1921)
 Collected Poems (Ed. C. Day Lewis) (1963)
SITWELL, Sir Osbert: 'Wilfred Owen' in Penguin *New Writing*, No 27,
 (April, 1946)
WELLAND, D. S. R.: *Wilfred Owen: a Critical Study* (1960)
 A Tribute to Wilfred Owen, compiled by T. J. Walsh (1964)
OWEN, Harold: *Journey from Obscurity I* and *II* (1963–4)
JONES, David: *In Parenthesis* (1937, 2nd, paperback, ed. 1963)
ROSENBERG, Isaac: *Collected Works* (Ed. Gordon Bottomley and D. Harding)
 (1937)
HULME, T. E.: *Speculations* (1924, 2nd ed. 1949)
ROBERTS, Michael: *T. E. Hulme* (1938)
Des Imagistes (1914)
Some Imagist Poets (1915)
POUND, Ezra: *Umbra* (Collected Early Poems) (1920)
 Hugh Selwyn Mauberley (1920)
 A Draft of XXX Cantos (1930)
 Selected Poems Ed. with Introduction by T. S. Eliot (1938)
KENNER, Hugh: *The Poetry of Ezra Pound* (1951)
LAWRENCE, D H.: *The Complete Poems* Ed. with Introduction and Notes by
 V. de S. Pinto and Warren Roberts (1964)
 Letters Ed. A. Huxley (1932)
HOUGH, Graham: *The Dark Sun* (1956)
ALVAREZ, A.: *The Shaping Spirit* (1958)
SAGAR, Keith: *The Art of D. H. Lawrence* (1966)

CHAPTER 7

CONRAD, Joseph: *The Secret Agent* (1907)
ELIOT, T. S.: *Prufrock and Other Observations* (1917)
 Anabasis a Poem by St J. Perse, with a Translation by T. S. Eliot (1930)
 Collected Poems 1909–1935 (1936)
 Murder in the Cathedral (1935)
 The Family Reunion (1939)

ELIOT, T. S.: *Four Quartets* (1944)
    The Sacred Wood (1920)
    For Lancelot Andrewes Essays on Style and Order (1928)
    Dante (1929)
    Selected Essays (1932)
    The Use of Poetry and the Use of Criticism (1933)
    After Strange Gods. A Primer of Modern Heresy (1937)
    The Music of Poetry (1942) (W. P. Ker Memorial lecture)
    Notes Towards the Definition of Culture (1948)
MATTHIESEN, F.: *The Achievement of T. S. Eliot* (1940)
RAJAN, B. (Editor): *T. S. Eliot, A Study of his Writings by Several Hands* (1948)
MARCH, R. and TAMBIMUTTU, T. (Editors): *T. S. Eliot: A Symposium* (1948)
HAMILTON, G. Rostrevor: *The Tell-Tale Article* (1949)
GARDNER, Helen: *The Art of T. S. Eliot* (1949)
Essays on Eliot in *Axel's Castle* by Edmund Wilson, *Abinger Harvest* by E. M. Forster, *New Bearings in English Poetry* by F. R. Leavis, *The Destructive Element* by Stephen Spender.

CHAPTER 8

GRAVES, R. and HODGE, Alan: *The Long Weekend—A Social History of Great Britain 1918–1939*
SPENDER, Stephen: 'The Life of Literature' (in *Partisan Review*, November, December 1948, January 1949)
HUXLEY, Aldous: *Antic Hay* (1923)
MAUGHAM, Somerset: *For Services Rendered* (1932)
Wheels, An Anthology of Verse (Six Cycles, 1916–1921)
SITWELL, Edith: *Collected Poems* (1931)
    Selected Poems (1936)
    I Live Under a Black Sun (1936)
    Street Songs (1942)
    Green Song (1944)
    A Poet's Notebook (1944)
    The Shadow of Cain (1947)
    The Song of the Cold (1946)
    'Some Notes on the Making of a Poem' (in *Orpheus I*, 1948)
    'On My Poetry' (in *Orpheus II*, 1948)
BOWRA C. M.: *Edith Sitwell* (1947)
CLARK, Sir K.: 'On the Development of Miss Sitwell's Later Style' (in *Horizon*, July 1947)
New Signatures: Poems by Several Hands (collected by Michael Roberts) (1932)
LEWIS, C. Day: *Collected Poems 1929–1933* (1935)
    A Time to Dance (1935)
    Overtures to Death (1938)
    The Georgics of Virgil (1940)
AUDEN, W. H.: *Poems* (1929)
    The Orators (1930)
    The Dog beneath the Skin (1935)
    Look Stranger (1936)

The Ascent of F6 (1936) } both in collaboration with C. Isherwood
On the Frontier (1938) }
HOGGART, R.: Auden: an Introductory Essay (1951)
    W. H. Auden (1957)
SPENDER, Stephen: Poems (1933)
    Vienna (1936)
    The Trial of a Judge (1938)
MAC NEICE, L.: Poems (1935)
    Out of the Picture (1937)
    The Earth Compels (1940)
    Selected Poems (1940)
AUDEN and MACNEICE: Letters from Iceland (1937)
BELL, Julian: Essays, Poems, and Letters (1938)
BARKER, George: Alanna Autumnal (1933)
    Thirty Preliminary Poems (1933)
    Calamiterror (1937)
    Poems (1935)
    Lament and Triumph (1940)
    Collected Poems 1930–1955 (1957)
GASCOYNE, David: Poems 1937–1942 (1943)
THOMAS, Dylan: Eighteen Poems (1934)
    Twenty-Five Poems (1936)
    The Map of Love (1939)
    Collected Poems 1934–1952 (1952)
For Dada, see Axel's Castle by Edmund Wilson, Appendix II
For Surrealism, see Surrealism edited by H. Read (1936)

INDEX

THE POLYTECHNIC OF WALES
LIBRARY
TREFOREST